The Gandhi-Jinnah Talks

The Gandhi-Jinnah Talks

Sheshrao Chavan

GNOSIS

Nurturing the Aspirations

Worldwide Circulation through Authorspress Global Network
First Published 2010
by
GNOSIS
E-35/103, Jawahar Park
Laxmi Nagar, Delhi-110 092
e-mail: authorspress@yahoo.com

An Imprint of Authorspress

The Gandhi-Jinnah Talks
ISBN 978-81-89012-99-1

Printed in India at Tarun Offset, Delhi.

Foreword

Sheshrao Chavan is a prolific writer of significance. He penned down a number of books of historical, social and judicial content and has written on eminent personalities of different disciplines and varied fields. He is constantly engaged in writing on themes that have a bearing on our present day condition. His book, *Mohammad Ali Jinnah—the Great Enigma,* translated into many Indian languages, should be particularly read for his objective outlook and treatment. His latest book, *The Gandhi–Jinnah Talks,* is again a book of different kind, which may serve as a catalyst for generating new thinking in the days to come. It is likely to inspire students of history for further studies in this direction.

The Gandhi-Jinnah Talks brings two great personalities face to face, discussing and analysing important issues of the times. It is a continual and sustained exercise in conversational mode. The mere fact that the two met and talked for full 18 days, prior to the making of Pakistan, shows how important the exercise was.

The Gandhi-Jinnah Talks, as presented here, covers historical, political, social and ethical aspects of a complex problem with a definite political agenda. It unfolds the religious, racial, social, political attitudes, the egos, the idiosyncrasies, the thought processes in the manifold stages of the dialogue.

It is a fact of history that in 1944, the political situation changed to a large measure and required a dialogue at the highest level. Gandhiji was quick to take note of it. So, he sought a dialogue with Jinnah. But what a paradox! In 1937-38, it was Jinnah who had requested Gandhiji for personal discussion with him on Hindu-Muslim problems. Gandhiji then took a little notice of Jinnah's request and asked him to contact Maulana Abul Kalam Azad in the first instance. Now, the wheel turned a full circle and it was Gandhiji who was seeking an interview with Jinnah. It would be interesting to note that the date, 9 September 1944, for beginning the talks was fixed as per the convenience of Jinnah.

The Gandhi-Jinnah talks were spread over 18 days, i.e., from 9 September to 27 September 1944. In between the talks, there were exchange of letters, explanations, clarifications, interspersed with report, discussions, press interviews, dialogues with the leaders. The Rajaji Formula and the Lahore Resolution were taken, one after another, as focal points for deliberating on the communal questions, the division of the country and the self-determination principle. Points, counter points, opinions, counter-opinions emerged during the talks. There were sharp exchanges, but the two leaders steadfastly adhered to their declared positions. They stuck to their earlier concepts of nation, nationality, race and religion. It was like two stalwarts countering each other's logic. Virtually, it turned out to be a battle of words and nerves. No doubt, it was a test of patience and perseverance for Gandhi as well as Jinnah. Gandhi felt that they seemed to be moving in a circle, but still he persisted with the talks in the hope that he might ultimately succeed in his mission. Both were logical, witty and hard in negotiations. There was no discernable shift in their stands. No meeting ground emerged. The talks left them dumb, breathless and exhausted. Hence the failure.

The text of the conversation has many layers of meanings which need to be connected, explored and reconstructed by the historians as well as by the students of history. The writer has humbly taken up the challenge to do so. Wherever he felt it necessary, he peeped into the layers and reviewed the processes underneath. At times, he synchronised his textual readings with views and reviews expressed by other leaders.

There was expectation by the general masses that the talks would be helpful in maintaining and balancing the Hindu-Muslim relationship. Gandhiji himself wished to create a bridge between the two communities, but the failure of the talks filled the air with disgust and disappointment and widened the gulf. Gandhiji's experience of three weeks negotiations confirmed his view that the presence of the third party, i.e., the British, hindered the solution of the communal problem. His view that Hindu-Muslim unity cannot be achieved without ousting the foreign ruling power, seems to be just and fair as borne out by later events.

Historically speaking, the talks (1944) are delicately placed in between the Quit India Movement (1942) and the Cabinet Mission Plan (1946). The talks directly or indirectly touch both the fringes. It is not just Rajaji's Formula but also the Lahore Resolution that have many a time been brought into the picture. Gandhiji's letter of 15 September to Jinnah says: "You do not claim to be a separate nation by right of conquest but by reason of acceptance of Islam. Will the two nations become one if the whole India accepted Islam? Will Bengalis, Oriyas, Andhras, Tamilians, Maharashtrians,

Gujaratis, etc., cease to have their special characteristics if all of them become converts to Islam?" Such questions that we come across in the talks are really eye-openers. Seen from this angle, the book is a document in conversation, which, in many respects, relates to our present- day problems.

The talks contain certain issues which have their relevance in our contemporary situation. The Hindu-Muslim question to which the two leaders addressed themselves is one of them. It haunted them during the talks. They had their own ways to deal with it then but unfortunately reached nowhere. Dealing with the Lahore Resolution, Gandhiji at one stage posed the question: "Is the goal of Pakistan Pan-Islam?" Today, the question haunts us all the more. Pan-Islamism, as referred to in the talks, has passed through many stages and it has now assumed dangerous proportions in the shape of regional and global terrorism. The sub-text of the talks can be studied in this respect. Conversion through conversation that Gandhiji always tried, along with developmental work in localised and regional trouble and terror spots can go a long way for resolving such conflicts. Likewise, a mix of Gandhian, military and diplomatic strategies, although look contradictory, may help us to combat and stem the global terrorism.

Sheshrao Chavan has very ably presented the day-to-day sequence, climax, anti-climax and of the talks. He has placed on record historical facts and documents in an impartial way. He leaves the reader to draw his own conclusions and form his own assessment. Imposing his views on readers or to be judgmental is not his way of writing, he strives for an open ending, not a closed one. His method is more exploratory than interpretative. He presents facts from all sides in a dispassionate and objective manner. Whenever, he chooses to interpret, he does it without fear or favour.

The Gandhi-Jinnah Talks is not only a book on an important phase of our contemporary history, but it reveals the facts of that period effortlessly. With utmost ease, Chavan explores the psyche of two great personalities who shaped the destinies of this subcontinent. It helps us to understand divergent opinions that surfaced in the talks and circumstances that led to partition. It captures vividly the historical moments in an intimate manner without losing sight of the political scenario of that period.

Dr. Narendra Mohan
Poet, Writer, Dramatist and Critic

Preface

Right from the beginning to the end of the talks, Jinnah remained adamant on his stand, that it was not possible to negotiate and reach an agreement unless both the parties were fully authoritatively represented. Jinnah refused to accept Gandhiji in his individual capacity, to which Gandhiji never agreed.

Jinnah refused to admit that the talks were as a result of Rajaji's correspondence with him and Gandhiji's consultation with the Muslim League Council. He reminded Gandhiji that the talks were entirely in response to his letter of 17 July 1944.

As the talks progressed the truth began to peep through that there was going to be no give but only take. Jinnah had come not to be convinced or even to discuss; the objections had been waved only to give the "seeker" a chance to receive the light and joined the band of the faithful.

Jinnah vehemently told Gandhiji: "We maintain and hold that Muslims and Hindus are two major nations by any definition or test of a nation. We are a nation of one hundred millions, and what is more, we are a nation with our own distinctive culture and civilization, language and literature, art and architecture, names and nomenclature, sense of value and proportion, legal laws and moral codes, customs and calendar, history and traditions, aptitude and ambitions; in short, we have our own, distinctive outlook on life and of life. By all canons of international law we are a nation."

Gandhiji's reaction to this statement of Jinnah was: "I am unable to accept the proposition that the Muslims of India are a nation, distinct from rest of the inhabitants of India. Mere assertion is no proof."

He further said: "I find no parallel in history for a body of converts and their descendents claiming to be a nation apart from the present stock. If India was one nation before the advent of Islam, it must remain one in spite of the change of the faith of a very large body of her children."

He continued: "You do not claim to be a separate nation by right of conquest, but by reason of acceptance of Islam. Will the two nations become one, if the whole of India accepted Islam?"

The talks thereafter, on Jinnah's part, entered upon an acrimonious phase. He even took exception to Gandhiji's saying that though he (Gandhiji) represented nobody, he aspired to represent all the inhabitants of India, because he realised in his own person their misery and degradation which is their common lot irrespective of class, caste or creed.

This was enough for Jinnah. Although he could go as far as to admit that Gandhiji was a great man, who was exercising enormous influence over the Hindus, particularly the masses, he could not accept that he aspired to represent all inhabitants. "It is quite clear that you represent nobody but the Hindus, and as long as you do not realize your true position, it is very difficult for me to argue with you," Jinnah told Gandhiji.

Gandhiji pleaded with Jinnah to consider how the independent States envisaged by him would materially or otherwise be benefited by being split up and whether independent States would not become a menace to themselves and to the rest of India. Jinnah's inflexible reply was that this was the only solution of the Indian problem and India must pay the price for its independence.

"The more our argument progresses, the more alarming your picture appears to me," wrote Gandhiji to Jinnah at the end of the first week of their talks. "As I imagine," Gandhiji further wrote, "in the working of the Lahore Resolution in practice, I see nothing but ruin for the whole of India."

This argument of Gandhiji also went on the deaf ears of Jinnah. And he insisted that Gandhiji should accept the basis and fundamental principles adumbrated in the Lahore resolution.

This forced Gandhiji to tell Jinnah: "I cannot accept the Lahore Resolution as you want me to, especially when you seek to introduce in its interpretation theories and claims, which I can neither accept nor can I ever hope to induce India to accept it."

"Can we not agree," Gandhiji finally pleaded, "to differ on the question of two nations and yet solve the problem on the basis of self-determination?"

Differing from the general basis proposed by Jinnah and the Muslim league of the two-nation theory, Gandhiji said, he could yet recommend to the Congress and the country acceptance of the claim for separation of those parts. If the majority of all the adult population of those parts voted in favour of separation, those areas would be formed into a separate State as soon as India was free.

Gandhiji called this division as between two brothers. Children of the same family, dissatisfied with one another by reason of change of religion, if they wished, could separate, but then the separation would be within themselves and not separation in the face of the whole world. When two brothers separate, they do not become enemies, one of the other in the eyes of the world. The world would still recognise them as brothers.

But Jinnah was not for separation on the basis of plebiscite. He wanted the issue to be decided on the basis of self-determination confined to the Muslims alone. He said: "Ours is a case of division and carving two independent sovereign States by way of settlement between two major nations, Hindus and Muslims, and not of severance or secession from any existing union which is *non est* in India."

Jinnah wanted separation to come first and a treaty for the safeguarding of common interests of India afterwards, on such terms as the two parts might agree to, or if they could agree. This, as the Congress President Maulana Abul Kalam Azad put, was like divorce before marriage.

Jinnah declined even to discuss Gandhiji's proposal saying: "It is difficult to deal with it any further unless it comes from you in your representative capacity."

Reacting to this, Gandhiji said: "Your constant references to my not being clothed with representative authority are really irrelevant.... If you break, it cannot be because I have no representative capacity or because I have been unwilling to give you satisfaction in regard to the claim embodied in the Lahore Resolution."

Shifting the blame to Gandhiji's door, Jinnah said: "If a break comes, it will be because you have not satisfied me in regard to the essence of the claim embodied in the Lahore Resolution....If a break comes, it will be most unfortunate. If one does not agree with you or differs from you, you are always right and the other party is always wrong, and the next thing is that many are waiting prepared in your circle to pillory me when the word goes, but I must face all threats and consequences, and I can only act according to my judgment and conscience."

When the talks reached the breaking point, Gandhiji suggested that he should be allowed to meet the Muslim League Council and if need be permitted to address the open session of the League. As an alternative he suggested that the issue may be referred to the arbitration.

But none of these suggestions was acceptable to Jinnah. He informed Gandhiji: "It is most extraordinary and an unprecedented suggestion to make. Only a member or a delegate is entitled to participate in the deliberations of the meeting of the Council or in the open session of the Muslim League."

Commenting on the posture taken by Jinnah, Pyarelal in his book, *Last Phase, Part 1* at page 93 writes: "It is not considered either extraordinary or unprecedented even for a sovereign Parliament to invite leaders and statesmen of another friendly country to come and address its members. Why was Jinnah so chary of allowing any contact to develop between Gandhiji and the Muslim League Council if his object was to explore avenues for a settlement between Hindus and Muslims? Was it because he was afraid that they might see reason where he had refused to? Or did he think the more the members of his camp were protected from the 'corrupting' influence of the Mahatma, the easier it would be for him to manage them as a docile body?"

Pyarelal further writes: "I was curious that when once during the negotiations, I invited members of Jinnah's personal staff to tea and a friendly chat with the members of Gandhiji's party, I received the following reply from his Secretary: 'I am sorry to inform you that it will not be possible for us to accept your kind invitation till the present talks are over.'"

Millions in India and outside had looked forward to the Gandhi-Jinnah talks as the beginning of a new chapter in the Hindu-Muslim relationship. But the talks failed, because, as Gandhiji put it, "A mind enslaved cannot act as if it were free. His experience of the three weeks negotiations had further confirmed in his view that the presence of the third party, i.e., British, hindered the solution of the communal problem."

The date-wise details of the Gandhi-Jinnah talks have been given in the book along with the opinions of the experts on the Rajaji Formula and the reactions of eminent persons on the Gandhi-Jinnah talks, which will help the readers to form their own opinion.

Sheshrao Chavan

Acknowledgements

Dr. Narendra Mohan had read my book, *Mohammad Ali Jinnah—the Great Enigma,* and profusely complemented me for following *Rajtarangini* of Kalhana and Jadunath Sarkar in presenting the facts. The substance of the Gandhi-Jinnah talks finds place in the book.

Dr. Narendra Mohan was in Aurangabad for three months in the second half of 2009 to study *Malik Ambar* with a view to produce a drama on him. He motivated me to bring out a book giving every possible detail of the Gandhi-Jinnah talks. I was reluctant, because of the book in my hand on Hindu-Muslim relations. I revealed to Dr. Narendra Mohan as to what was boiling in my mind about the attitude developed by Muslims in India after three decades of independence.

Dr. Narendra Mohan in his style convinced me to defer the book in my hand and give priority to the Gandhi-Jinnah talks, which he has termed as 18 Chapters of the *Bhagavad Gita* in his drama, *Mr Jinnah.*

Experiencing the rare qualities of dedication, devotion and commitment to the cause in Dr. Narendra Mohan during his stay in Aurangabad, I was left with no alternative, but to yield to him. This, of course, I did on the condition that he would write, *Foreword* to the book.

I would not have gone into the details of the Gandhi-Jinnah talks, but for Dr. Narendra Mohan. I extend my gratitude to him for this and for his Foreword.

I have been encouraged and helped in my endeavour by Hon'ble Justice Chandrashekhar Dharmadhikari, Shri Dhirubhai Mehta, Shri A.N. Kadam, Dr. Mangala Vaishnav and Dr. J.S. Sardar. I am grateful to them.

My grand daughter, Miss Nikita and grandson, Master Anurag, have always been of assistance to me in computer work. I thank both of them with appreciation.

I told Sudarshan Kcherry on 13 December 2009 that my manuscript on the Gandhi-Jinnah Talks was ready and whether he would publish the book. His instant reply was "Why not?"

Shri Sudarshan is a spiritual person. He has published a number of my earlier books in record time and that too without compromise on the quality. This book has also seen the light of day in record time, for which I profusely thank Sudarshan Kcherry of Authorspress.

Sheshrao Chavan

Contents

1

The Background of the Talks

Mahatma Gandhi's personality was the rallying point of all shades of revolutionary groups, even if all of them were not in favour of non-violence. Methods might differ, but for the goal of independence, the Mahatma was a symbol of determination. His 'Quit India' message was likewise the rallying cry for all those who wanted to end the Raj. Having fought violent battles against the British near Cox's Bazar on Indian soil, in the China Hills and the Naga Hills, having captured Kohima where the tricolour flag was hoisted, and having advanced into the plains of Imphal, Netaji Subhash Chandra Bose, too, had thought of Gandhi as a supreme messiah of Indian revolution, and the fountainhead of inspiration to all.

Addressing an appeal to him over the radio on 6 July 1944, he said: Mahatmaji! ... For Indians outside India, you are the creator of the present awakening in our country. The high esteem in which you are held by patriotic Indians outside India and by foreign friends of India's freedom, was increased a hundredfold when you bravely sponsored the 'Quit India' Resolution in August 1942...India's last war of independence has begun. Troops of Azad Hind Fauz are now fighting bravely on the soil of India, and in spite of all difficulty and hardship, they are pushing forward slowly but steadily.... Father of our nation! In this holy war for India's liberation we ask your blessings and good wishes.

The heroic advance of Netaji Subhash Chandra Bose, of course, came to a halt when the tide of the World War turned. But Gandhi's struggle had no end till the goal was reached. Aware of how his two formidable adversaries were working against India and the Congress, he thought of opening negotiations with them to make them see reason.

On 17 July 1944, he wrote to his first adversary Churchill: Dear Prime Minister, you are reported to have a desire to crush the 'simple naked Fakir' as you have said to have described me. I have been long trying to be a fakir and that naked—a more difficult task. The beauty of it for me and the pity of it for you is that no one can crush a satyagrahi; for, he offers his body as a willing sacrifice and thus makes the spirit free. I, therefore, regard the expression as a compliment though unintended. I approach you then as such and ask you to trust and use me for the sake of your people and mine and through them those of the world.

Pyarelal explains: "This letter to Churchill miscarried. It was the first instance in Gandhiji's experience of an important letter of his failing to reach its destination. A copy was, therefore, sent to Churchill. The only reply it fetched was an acknowledgement with thanks through the Viceroy."

Gandhiji's second adversary, Jinnah, in his Presidential address to the annual Session of the Muslim League at Delhi on April 24, 1943, said: "that nobody would welcome it more than he, if Gandhiji was really willing to come to a settlement with the Muslim League on the basis of Pakistan. If he has made up his mind what is there to prevent Mr. Gandhi from writing to me direct? I cannot believe that the government will have daring to stop such a letter if it is sent to me. It would be a very serious thing if such a letter were stopped.... If there is any change of heart, he has to drop a few lines to me. Then the Muslim League will not fail. But I do not see any kind of change on the part of Gandhi or the Congress or the Hindu leadership."

Gandhiji wrote a letter on 4 May 1943 to Jinnah in which he said: "When sometime after my incarceration, the government asked me for a list of newspapers I would like to have, I included the *Dawn* in my list. I have been receiving it with more or less regularity. Whenever it comes to me, I read it carefully. I have followed the proceedings of the League as reported in the *Dawn* columns. I noted your invitation to me to write to you. Hence this letter.

"I welcome your invitation. I suggest our meeting face to face rather than our talking through correspondence. But I am in your hands. I hope that this letter will be sent to you and if you agree to my proposal, that the Government will let you visit me.

"One thing I had better mention. There seems to be an 'if' about your invitation. Do you say I should write only if I have changed my heart? God alone knows men's hearts. I would like you to take me as I am.

"Why should not both you and I approach the great question of communal unity as men determined on finding a common solution and work together to make our solution acceptable to all who are concerned with or interested in it?"

It may be recollected that in 1937-38, Jinnah had repeatedly requested Gandhiji for personal discussion with him on Hindu-Muslim problems. Gandhiji then took little notice of Jinnah's request and asked him to contact Maulana Abul Kalam Azad in the first instance. Now the wheel turned full circle and it was Gandhij who was seeking an interview with Jinnah.

The Government did not forward Gandhiji's letter to Jinnah. However, E.Conran-Smith from the Home Department informed Gandhiji of the Government's decision to withhold the letter to Jinnah. He also drew Gandhiji's attention to an advance copy of the Government's press communiqué of May 26, which he had enclosed. The communiqué stated: "The Government of India have received a request from Mr. Gandhi to forward a short letter from himself to Mr. Jinnah expressing a wish to meet him. In accordance with their known policy in regard to correspondence or interview with Mr. Gandhi, the Government of India have decided that this letter cannot be forwarded and have so informed Mr. Gandhi and Jinnah. They are not prepared to give facilities for political correspondence or contact to a person detained for promoting an illegal mass movement which he has not disavowed, and thus gravely embarrassing India's war effort at a critical time. It rests with Mr. Gandhi to satisfy the Government of India that he can safely be allowed once more to participate in the public affairs of the country, and until he does so, the disabilities from which he suffers are his own choice."

The Viceroy was however, of the view that the letter should be forwarded and that Jinnah, if he wished to meet Gandhi, should be allowed to do so. (*Collected Works of Mahatma Gandhi,* Vol. 77, pp. 76-77)

Though Linlithgow favoured their meeting, Churchill wanted no Gandhi-Jinnah talks to upset his own summit with Franklin Roosevelt.

The Government, however, made the substance of Gandhiji's letter available to Jinnah. Thereupon, Jinnah declared that this was not the kind of letter which he had wanted from Gandhi. He wanted Gandhi first to agree to the Muslim League demand for partition and then write to him. "This letter of Mr. Gandhi can only be construed as a move on his part to embroil the Muslim League to come into clash with the British Government solely for the purpose of his release," said Jinnah.

(*Mahatma Gandhi: The Last Phase,* Pyarelal, pp.68-70)

On 27 May, Gandhiji wrote the following to Sir Richard Tottenham: "I received last evening your letter refusing my request to forward my letter addressed to Qaid-e-Azam Jinnah. I wrote only yesterday to the Superintendent of this camp asking him kindly to inquire whether my letter to Qaid-e-Azam, and later, the one dated 15 instant to Rt. Hon. Lord Samuel had been forwarded to the respective addresses.

"I am sorry for the Government's decision. For my letter to the Qaid-e-Azam was sent in reply to his public invitation to me to write to him, and I was especially encouraged to do so because his language had led me to think that if I wrote to him, my letter would be forwarded to him. The public too are anxious that the Qaid-e-Azam and I should meet or at least establish contact. I have always been anxious to meet the Qaid-e-Azam if perchance we could devise some solution of the communal tangle which might be generally acceptable. Therefore, the disability in the present instance is much more that of the public than mine. As a satyagrahi, I may not regard as disabilities the restrictions which the Government have imposed upon me. As the Government are aware, I have denied myself the pleasure of writing to my relatives as I am not allowed to perform the service of writing to my co-workers who are in the sense more to me than my relatives.

"The advance copy of the contemplated communiqué with which you have considerably favoured me requires emendation in more places than one. For, as it stands, it does not square with facts.

"As to the disavowal referred to in the present communiqué, the Government are aware that I regard the non-violent mass movement, for the launching of which the Congress gave me the authority on the 8 August last, as perfectly legitimate and in the interest of the Government and the public. As it is, the Government left me no time to start the movement. Therefore, how a movement, which was never started, could embarrass India's war efforts? If then, there was any embarrassment by reason of the popular resentment of the Government's action in resorting to the wholesale arrests of the principal Congressmen, the responsibility was solely that of the Government. The mass movement, as the resolution sanctioning it said in so many words, was sanctioned in order to promote India-wide effort on behalf of the allied cause, including the cause of Russia and China, whose danger was very great in August last and from which, in my opinion, they are by no means free even now. I hope the Government will not feel offended when I say that all the war effort that is being put forth in India is not India's but the alien Government's. I submit that if the Government had complied with the request of the Congress as embodied in its August resolution, there would have been a mass effort without parallel for winning the battle of human freedom and ridding the world of the menace that Fascism, Nazism, Japanism and Imperialism are. I may be wholly wrong; any way, this is my deliberate and honest opinion.

"In order to make the communiqué accord facts, suggest the following alteration in the first paragraph. After Mr. Jinnah add 'in response to his public invitation to Mr. Gandhi to write to him stating that he (Gandhi) would be willing to correspond with or meet him according as he wished.'

"I hope the remaining portion of the communiqué too will be suitably amended in the light of my submission."

Conran Smith informed Gandhiji: "The Government of India have considered it, but see no reason to modify their communiqué already published."

Release of Mahatma Gandhi

The conference or the Council of Dominion Prime Ministers met in London under the presidentship of Winston Churchill from 1 to 16 May 1944. On behalf of India, Feroz Khan Noon and the Maharaja of Kashmir attended the conference as members of the Viceroy's Council. While the conference was in session, Gandhiji was released on 6 May 1944 at 8 p.m. unconditionally.

Gandhiji had spent one year, nine months and 27 days in Yervada Jail.

"Personally," noted the Viceroy, "I could not see that we gained much credit by releasing him at the point of death; and if he was not at the point of death there was no need of such hurry. He satisfied himself on the report of his advisers resting on the findings of the doctors that Gandhi would not be a factor in active politics again. It was understood that his memory and headpiece may be affected."

After his release, Gandhiji took rest for three days in Poona at Premila Thackersy's mansion and then went to

Bombay, where he stayed with Shanti Kumar and Sumati Morarji in Palm Bun at Juhu Beach.

To rebuild his health, Gandhiji went to Panchgani, a hill station near Poona. Rajaji joined him there at Gandhiji's insistence.

Gandhiji recovered quickly to make himself active again. To the Congressmen who were still free, Gandhiji's presence outside at once brought a renewed confidence. The mass awakening in the wake of the revolution had moved the consciousness of the country in radically new directions. Whether the Congress had acted correctly or gone wrong at places in the course of a leaderless revolution was a point of no significance. That the people had shown great courage, endured suffering and sacrifice, faced death boldly in the struggle was a matter of pride for all. "The August resolution is still there," Gandhi told Congressmen. "I cannot alter, nor do I wish to alter, a single comma in that resolution....Nor hair-splitting discussions are called for. One step is enough."

On 17 June 1944, Gandhiji asked permission to see the Viceroy and the members of the Congress Working Committee. Following instructions from the War Cabinet, Wavell replied to Gandhiji that he saw no point in meeting him. His national Government proposal, the Viceroy added, was unacceptable even as a basis for discussion.

During discussions in London and between London and New Delhi, on the reply to be sent to Gandhiji, Churchill had said to his war cabinet: "I hope the cabinet will stand firm. As a matter of fact, the Viceroy has no right to negotiate with Gandhi at all, considering he was responsible for passing to us the medical opinion on which we were told that he would never be able to take part in politics again." Churchill added that he objected to any impression of a great parley between the Viceroy and the newly released invalid.

Gandhiji's renewed activities for confrontation with the British when the war presented prospects of success for the allies annoyed Winston Churchill so greatly that he was at his wit's end as to how to deal with his arch enemy. When the Viceroy was pressing hard upon the Prime Minister for the shipment of food to India to save millions of lives in Bengal, and was eagerly awaiting a telegram in that connection, he was surprised to receive instead Churchill's peevish telegram, dated 5 July 1944, asking why Gandhi had not yet died! No Viceroy could have devised an answer to this. (*A Centenary History of Indian National Congress,* B.N Pande, pp. 62-63)

Gandhiji gave an interview to Stuart Gilder, a British journalist and a special war correspondent of the *News Chronicle* on 9 July 1944.

The substance of the interview was that Gandhiji could do nothing without consulting the Congress Working Committee. If he met the Viceroy, he would tell him that it was his purpose to help and not hinder the Allied war effort. He had no intention of offering civil disobedience. History could never be repeated; he could not take the country back to 1942. The world had moved on during the last two years and the whole situation had to be reviewed *de novo.* Today, he would be satisfied with a national government in full control of civil administration and would advise the Congress to participate in such a government if formed.

Stuart Gilder, who again interviewed Gandhiji on 17 July at Panchgani, sent a cable to *News Chronicle,* in which about the Rajaji Formula he said: "Mr. Gandhi has also approved the proposals submitted to Mr. Jinnah by Mr.

Rajagopalachari, which agree to a solution of the Hindu-Muslim dispute by a plebiscite and demarcation of the districts where Muslims are in a majority, if Muslim League will endorse the demand for independence and cooperate with the Congress in the formation of a provisional government for the transitional period."

Gilder further said: "If the Muslim League accepts Mr. Rajagopalachari's proposals and the government will now discuss the situation with Mr. Gandhi, the deadlock can be solved and a new page opened in Indian history. Mr. Gandhi pointed out that he had no authority to speak in the name of the Congress without consulting the Working Committee, but there is no doubt whatever that his views and the Hindu-Muslim proposals as endorsed by him would be accepted by them without hesitation." (*Collected Works of Mahatma Gandhi,* Vol. 77, p. 474)

On 27 July 1944, Gandhiji wrote to Lord Wavell to the effect that he was prepared to advise the Congress Working Committee to renounce mass civil disobedience and to give full cooperation in the war effort, if a declaration of immediate Indian independence were made and a national government responsible to the Central Assembly were formed, subject to the proviso that during the pendency of the war, military operations should continue as at present, but without any financial burden upon India.

The very next day on 28 July, the Secretary of State in his speech on India Debate in the House of Commons, said that Gandhi's proposals obviously did not form even the staring point for profitable discussions, either with Lord Wavell or with the interned Congress leaders.

Gandhiji wrote to Jinnah on 17 July 1944 addressing him as 'Brother Jinnah' and signing the letter as your brother Gandhi. In the letter Gandhiji said: "There was a time when I was able to persuade you to speak in our mother tongue. Today, I venture to write in the same. I had already invited you, while I was in jail. After my release I have not written to you. I am prompted to do so. Let us meet when you wish. Please do not regard me as an enemy of Islam and the Muslims here. I have always been a servant and friend of yours and the whole world. Do not dismiss me. I am enclosing a translation of this letter in Urdu."

Gandhiji's request was a striking contrast to the high and mighty attitude displayed by Jawaharlal Nehru in rejecting Jinnah's offer of coalition ministry in 1937. Six years had indeed wrought a change in the balance of power in Indian politics.

Jinnah replied to Gandhi on 24 July 1944: "I shall be glad to receive you at my residence in Bombay on my return from Srinagar, which will be about the middle of August. I would like to say nothing more till we meet."

(*Collected Works of Mahatma Gandhi*, Vol. 77, p. 394)

Jinnah was, however, required to postpone his meeting because of his lung infecton.

In his statement issued on 5 August 1944 from Sevagram, Gandhiji said: "God may bless the Qaid-e-Azam and me with wisdom to reach a common understanding in the interest of India."

A deputation led by Mr. Ibadat Yar Khan and consisting of Sir Ziauddin Ahmed, Mahomad Ashfaq, Amiruddin Alvi and A.M.Safi met Gandhiji on 15 August 1944 and urged for an honourable settlement between the Muslim League and the Congress in the meeting of the two great leaders of the Hindus and the Muslims. Gandhiji showed his willingness to concede every reasonable demand of the Musalmans and said: "I want that myself and Qaid-e-Azam should be locked up and should not be allowed to come out till we come to some decision to remove the deadlock."

The members of the deputation again requested Gandhiji to end the deadlock and see India governed by Indians themselves, for which he had been trying for such a long time, Gandhiji replied: "I wish to see a free India in my life time, for God knows what will happen when I am no more."

M.R. Jayakar wrote a letter to Gandhiji on 17 August in which he said: "I wish you all success in your efforts, although I feel more or less certain that, between the arrogance of the Government of India and the equal arrogance of the Muslim League leader, your work is very difficult, if not impossible with all differences of views. I wish you success in your magnificent undertaking."

In reply Gandhiji informed Jayakar that for the moment the meeting has been delayed owing to the Qaid-e-Azam's illness.

Gandhiji sent a telegram to Jinnah on 18 August saying, "Your phone and wire. Deeply grieved. Hope you will soon recover. Anxiously await further news."

The telegram was followed by a letter on the same day in which Gandhiji said: "How was it that you fell ill all of a sudden? The whole world was looking for our meeting. I had entertained high hopes, although, I must admit, I had my own apprehensions. Hence when Fatimabehen (Jinnah's sister) conveyed to me the news of your illness, I was shaken. I hope God will soon restore you to health, hasten the meeting to which the whole world is looking forward and that the meeting will lead to the welfare of India.

"I hope Fatimabehn or some one else will keep me informed about your health."

Gandhiji gave an interview to the Associated Press of India on 18 August 1944 at Sevagram in which among other things, he said: "It is most unfortunate that at this critical juncture the Qaid-e-Azam has fallen ill and under medical advice cannot see me till he is free from his illness. A proper heart-agreement between us can induce a revision of the firm refusal of the British Government as conveyed through His Excellency's letter. Let us all pray that the Qaid-e-Azam may be soon restored enough to see me and that God may so dominate our hearts as to lead us to a right solution."

Addressing Jinnah as 'Bhai' (subsequently all letters were addressed as 'Bhai'), Gandhiji in his letter of 23 August said: "I learn from the newspapers that your fever has gone down. Thank God. But you continue to be weak and the doctors have advised visitors not to insist on appointments just yet. I had your letter yesterday. May Allah grant you early and complete recovery. I do not want you to hurry for my sake. Only I can fix up my time for other work and for visitors if you inform me the earliest possible date for our meeting. I shall be grateful if you ask someone to intimate this to me through a letter, a telephone call or a telegram."

Gandhiji sent a letter to Jinnah on 29 August in which he wrote: "I got neither a telegram nor a letter by the return of post. That made me impatient and I sent the telegram. Afterwards I got your reply. Thanks. I am glad to learn that you are keeping well.

"I have fixed my engagements up to the 7 September. I have kept myself free after that date. Hence I can present myself on or after 9, whenever you call me."

Jinnah informed Gandhiji on 30 August that 7 September or any day thereafter would suit him.

In reply Gandhiji informed Jinnah on 31 August: "I have your telegram. Thanks. I had written a letter to you on the 29 . You must have got it. As mentioned in it I have already fixed up appointments with various people up to the 7. I can, therefore, start from here (Sevagram) on 8 September at the earliest and reach there on the 9 . I hope the day will suit you. If it does, kindly let me know."

Gandhiji also sent a telegram to Jinnah saying: "Reaching you four o'clock ninth." He also informed B.G. Kher on 1 September that he was reaching Bombay on the 9 to meet Qaid-e-Azam.

Talk with Students' Delegation

The students, led by Hari Prasanna Mishra, General Secretary of the All-India Hindu Students Federation, picketed Gandhiji's hut in Sevagram on 6 September 1944. The following dialogue took place between them and Gandhiji: H.P.Mishra: We won't like your seeing Mr. Jinnah as you are likely to be duped and the Hindus are likely to be exploited by Mr. Jinnah at our cost. Gandhiji: I will not ignore or compromise a single interest, be sure.

Students from Bengal who requested Gandhiji not to decide on a settlement were asked by the Mahatma:

"Have I not done any good for Hindus?"

Hari Prasanna Mishra questioned Gandhiji whether he accepted responsibility for what was going on in Bengal resulting from the Communal Award. To this Gandhiji replied: How can I? The Bengal students requested Gandhiji to leave the communal question to the Sabha and the League.

Gandhiji assured the students that he would not do anything without consulting Bengal. Despite these assurances, the students informed Gandhiji of their intention to continue picketing and Gandhiji replied: "If you thus prevent me, I will have to wire Mr. Jinnah that I am arrested and so postpone the meeting."

Two followers of V.D. Savarkar, namely, Nathuram Godse and L.G. Thatte, went from Poona to Sevagram with the announced aim of physically preventing Gandhiji from leaving for Bombay. Accompanied by supporters, the pair arrived at the Ashram entrance, where the police asked them to have their say and disperse.

On their refusal to leave, Godse and Thatte were arrested. A dagger was found on Thatte, who said that a martyr would kill Gandhi. When a policeman asked whether such matters should not be left to a leader like Savarkar, Thatte replied: "That will be too great an honor for Gandhiji; adding that his companion (Godse) will be quite enough for the purpose."

In a letter to Sir Tej Bahadur Sapru, Pyarelal in his book, *Last Phase, Vol. 1* at page 82 writes:

"You must have seen in the papers a report of the doings of the Hindu Mahasabha picketers at Sevagram. On the first day the leader of the batch had blurted out that this was only the first step and, if necessary, force would be used to prevent Bapu from going to meet Jinnah. Yesterday they gave intimation that they would physically prevent him from going out of the hut, and planted pickets at all the three exit leading out of the hut.

"This morning, I had an intimation on the telephone from the District Superintendent of Police that they intended serious mischief, and, therefore, the police would be compelled to take action. Bapu had proposed to go all alone in their midst and proceed to Wardha (railway station) on foot unless they themselves changed their mind and asked him to get into the car.... Just before his departure, the D.S.P. came and said that he had arrested the picketers after giving them due notice, when all persuasion had failed.

"The leader of the picketers appeared to be very high strung, fanatical and of a neurotic type, which caused some anxiety. Searching of his person after arrest revealed a full-sized dagger. When the police officer who arrested him banteringly remarked that at any rate he (the picketer) had had the satisfaction of becoming a martyr, quick came the reply, "No, that will be when someone assassinates Gandhiji." "Why not leave it to the leaders to settle it among themselves? For instance, Savarkar (the Hindu Mahasabha leader) might come and do the job," jocularly remarked the police officer in question. The reply was, "That will be too great an honor for Gandhiji. The *jamadar* will be quite enough for the purpose."

2

The Rajaji Formula

After detaching himself from the Congress, C. Rajagopalachari was ploughing a lonely furrow, with little hope of raising a political crop. Early in November 1943, he had talks with Jinnah. He seems to have found him in a cooperative mood, in which he was almost inclined to be constructive about the future. The impression left on Rajaji was that there was only a small gap to be bridged. On 12 November 1943, he saw the Viceroy, acquainted him with the change in Jinnah's attitude and sought his permission to see and consult Gandhiji. The Viceroy, however, refused to him his permission.

Soon after, Rajaji also made an offer to go to England if he were given facilities to do so. The Secretary of State saw no advantage to be gained from such a visit. He said in the House of Commons that while the Government welcomed Rajaji's endeavours to promote an agreed settlement of the Indian problem, it was clear that any such agreement must come about in India between the Indian parties.

Jinnah was distrustful of Rajaji's moves. The Scheduled Caste leaders were also critical. Dr. B.R. Ambedkar said: "Mr Rajagopalachari seems to feel like an orphan in the storm keenly feeling for the kith and kin whom he deserted in search of green pastures. Nobody can accept his proposals."

Rajagopalachari was convinced that there was no escape from some form of partition of the country if there were to be any progress in the constitutional field. Earlier, in 1943, he had drawn up a formula to serve as a basis for a settlement between the Congress and the Muslim League. He had shown it to Gandhiji and obtained his approval when he had been allowed to see him during his fast in February of that year. Now, in April 1944, he communicated the formula to Jinnah and had discussions and correspondence with him. The terms of the formula which Rajaji published on 10 July were as follows:

1. Subject to the terms set out below as regards the constitution for free India, the Muslim League endorses the Indian demand for independence and will co-operate with the Congress in the formation of a provincial interim Government for the transitional period.

2. After the termination of the war, a commission shall be appointed for demarcating contiguous districts in the north-west and east of India, wherein the Muslim population is in absolute majority. In the areas thus demarcated, a plebiscite of all the inhabitants held on the basis of adult suffrage or other practicable franchise shall ultimately decide the issue of separation from Hindustan. If the majority decide in favor of forming a sovereign State separate from Hindustan, such decision shall be given effect to without prejudice to the right of districts on the border to choose to join either State.

3. It will be open to all parties to advocate their points of view before the plebiscite is held.

4. In the event of separation, mutual agreement shall be entered into for safeguarding defence, and commerce and communications and for other essential purposes.
5. Any transfer of population shall only be on an absolutely voluntary basis.
6. These terms shall be binding only in case of transfer by Britain of full power and responsibility for the governance of India.

Jinnah, however, refused to have any direct communication with Rajaji. He questioned his authority to send the proposals, and said that if Gandhi were to send these proposals, he would place them before the Working Committee of the Muslim League. To this Rajaji in a telegram from Panchgani replied that Gandhiji had approved his formula, and if Jinnah still insisted on a direct proposal from him then it would be necessary to take the public into confidence before directly approaching Jinnah. Jinnah was adamant and reiterated that he had to place any proposal received on behalf of the Congress before the Working Committee of the League. Rajaji released his correspondence to the press along with the salient features of his formula on 10 July 1944.

In answer to a question on 15 July 1944 sent by London office of the United Press of India, Gandhiji replied: "Neither the Qaid-e-Azam nor the Muslim League pronounced their opinion on the Rajaji Formula. I would deprecate anticipating them. Rajaji is with me (Panchgani). We have agreed for the sake of conserving my limited energy that he should deal with the questions arising from the formula. In his press conference on 19." July 1944, Gandhiji said: "Rajaji's offer has seen the light of the day only now, but I had personally subscribed to it when I was fasting in prison camp. It is now 16 months old. For, the rest of the offer, I must carry out the contract between Rajaji and myself. He is to bear the brunt of all criticism that might be made about that offer."

In answer to a question on 20 July, Gandhiji again said: "Rajaji's Formula indicates my way of meeting the communal difficulty. I am indifferent whether it is called Pakistan." (*Collected Works of Mahatma Gandhi,* Vol 77, pp. 405, 411)

In his interview to the press on 30 July 1944, at Panchgani, Gandhiji said: "I expect to meet the Qaid-e-Azam as soon as he wants me, of course, health permitting. The publication of the Rajaji Formula is in pursuit of negotiations for a communal settlement. It is not an idle effort. It is conceived in all sincerity. It is unfortunate that the criticism that has been levelled against it, so far as I can see, has been conceived out of prejudice or careless study of the Formula. Nor is it an offer on the part of any party. It is a contribution from two life-servants of the nation towards the solution of the communal tangle, which has hitherto defined solution. The Rajaji Formula is intended as a help to lovers of the country. It is the best we could conceive, but it is open to amendments, as it is open to rejection or acceptance." (*Collected Works of Mahatma Gandhi,* Vol. 77, pp.439-40)

The Working Committee of the Muslim League which met on 30 July 1944, gave Jinnah full authority to negotiate with Gandhiji. He dismissed the Rajaji Formula as offering a shadow and a husk, a maimed, mutilated and moth-eaten Pakistan.

3

Opinions on the Rajaji Formula

Dr. K.M. Munshi, sent his reaction to Gandhiji through his letter of 9 August 1944. Munshi in his letter said:

"According to my humble opinion:

1. Akhand Hindustan is a fundamental principle for me. I am unable to change anything in it.
2. Whatever the constitution, only the areas having Muslim majority in India should constitute separate units. We cannot reconcile ourselves till the Punjab and Bengal are not partitioned.
3. It does not seem probable that the policy of Hindu-Muslim unity which has been a failure for the past 25 years will now succeed.
4. Today, none but the Muslims are honestly welcoming the Rajaji formula. You are of course powerful. There would be many who, for several reasons, would accept whatever you say. But what is rankling in their hearts would no doubt continue to do so.
5. By supporting the Rajaji formula, you have been able to prove your readiness to arrive at a communal settlement.

6. Jinnah's ambition of 25 years to determine the future of India in partnership with you is fulfilled. He is now convinced that the British are out to hit at him at Punjab, and so, he is eager to arrive at some settlement. If the settlement arrived at is such that it could be misused or if there is a deadlock, the situation is likely to be worse, than it was. I am so disturbed about this thing that I am relieving my burden by expressing myself to you. If, in your opinion, I should publish my view point in the proper form, do kindly let me know. I shall prepare and send it for your prior approval."

Gandhiji sent his following note to Munshi with his eldest son Jagdish Munshi:

1. Division of India is like poison to my mind; because I am also of the view that it is sinful to do so.
2. The Delhi resolution of 2 April was concerned with self-determination. After this on 30 April, Rajaji's resolution was turned down and Jagatnarayan's resolution about not partitioning India was adopted. In my view this was a highly inappropriate and hasty step and due to this alone Jinnah has been able to spread poison in the Muslim masses.
3. I had discussed this matter with Maulana (Azad) also. According to him, in spite of Jagatnarayan's resolution, I still retain the authority to discuss the matter with Jinnah because the resolution of 2 April still stands.
4. Later on when I had negotiations with Jinnah, I had asked him whether he would accept help from a foreign power, if he was granted a sovereign state. To this he said "Yes."

I th en asked him, if after securing that help, he would invade India. To this also he said, "Yes."

Then I told him: "It would be a sin to do such a thing and I cannot be a party to it."

5. Rajaji's offer does not seem to have the virulence of his earlier talk and hence I am in agreement with it. According to this offer if there can be a separate treaty regarding Defence, Foreign Affairs and Communications, I do not see any harm in giving him the rest. And after this, Pakistan seems to have no meaning at all.
6. Jinnah has complete faith in me. He knows that I have no axe to grind in these negotiations. And he seems to have somewhat softened by my last letters, and hence, my only advice can be that at such a time, nobody should create any obstacles. Jinnah has hated me since the day I asked him in a meeting to give up English and speak in Gujarati.
7. Jinnah is definitely not unselfish. He is prone to be easily led by others because of his vanity. (Just) because I am going to meet him, I am not led away by him. I have not accepted everything that he has said. Otherwise it would mean that he has won me around. That is why even when I meet him it will be with some misgivings.
8. I wish to conquer even Jinnah with trust and love. I have no other weapons at all.

Gandhiji sent his letter of 12 August 1944 to Munshi in which he said: "The moment I felt that Pakistan of Jinnah's imagination was sinful, I started believing in the Congress principle of self-determination. I would find no fault at all if you oppose without any fear Rajaji's formula. Where the intentions are honest, fear of public blame has no place at all. Possibly, your statement will not be ready by the time I meet Jinnah. But if you have prepared it, do send it. I shall go through it. If it needs to be improved or changed, I shall do so. Have no fear. I shall not do anything hastily. If you have time and if you think it is necessary, meet Rajaji and me. And I think it will be absolutely necessary to meet after our interview."

Munshi sent his reply to Gandhiji through his letter of 14 August 1944 in which he categorically stated: "I do not see that (your) meeting with Jinnah is going to lead anywhere. Francis Low, Editor of *Times of India*, met me today. He is haughty beyond words. He says, that the British Government has accepted Pakistan through Cripps and the Congress has done it through Gandhi. Now it is only a question of working out the details.

"I for one feel that the Hindu-Muslim clash will be prolonged affair. And I can see that by accepting an unstable settlement, we are likely to land ourselves in a situation worse than the present." (*Pilgrimage to Freedom*, K.M.Munshi, pp. 437-41)

Munshi's Unpublished Statement Sent to Gandhiji for Approval

Munshi, in his unpublished statement sent to Gandhiji for approval says:

"My reluctance to comment on the Rajaji formula has led to my attitude being misunderstood by many friends all over the country. But so far back as November 1942, I was permitted to place my views before the Working Committee of the Hindu Mahasabha at Delhi on the terms which Raja Maheshwar Dayal had brought from Mr. Jinnah. I then stressed the need of a dual policy: First, to stiffen the national resistance to Pakistan; Secondly; to concede the predominantly Muslim areas the right to form separate units and to enjoy autonomy in fullest measure consistently with the integrity of India in the international sphere; and lastly, to accept the principle of transfer of population so as to make both areas as far as practical homogeneous.

"My objections to the Rajaji Formula, however, go deeper. The old slogan was Hindu-Muslim unity to win Swaraj. Now it is Hindu-Muslim unity to win independence to achieve Pakistan. The old slogan failed; the new one, I am sure, will fail. Experience has shown that concession wrung alternately from the Nationalists and the British, has been one wave rolling after another towards the goal which is visible to all except those who do not wish to see. Mr. Jinnah only rides on the crest of the nearest wave. The force behind disruptions is the urge to convert Islam in India into a religio-political party and to dominate the country by overawing the Nationalists into submission. This force has rendered Gandhiji's life effort at Hindu-Muslim unity barren. The Lucknow Pact died the moment separate electorates were conceded. The Congress-Khilafat alliance failed, when the Muslims found that their objective of preserving Khilafat was no longer attainable. Mr. Jinnah's recent utterances are too fresh to be forgotten easily. He will accept no alliance on a conditional acceptance of Pakistan in the Formula, and if any is made it will not last a day after the principle of Pakistan is accepted by the Nationalists.

"My second objection is that the Destructionists will not rest content merely with the districts in which the Muslims predominate. They want *lebensraum* of predominately Hindu areas. *The Dawn* has already started sneering at Rajaji's proposals of division by districts. And if a civil war has to be avoided no district in which one community predominates should be placed in the area, of the other. If there are two nations, Sudation districts can only be retained at the peril of the both.

"My third objection is still more fundamental. I can conceive of a federation of predominantly Hindu and Muslim provinces; of a federation in which the Centre enjoys control of the federating Muslim Provinces only as regards strictly federal subjects. In such a federation conceivably there may be sub-federations, the third being that of Indian States. But the division of India into sovereign States is an unreal basis for a political settlement. As a day dream it is dangerous. In practice it is unrealisable. The Indian Princes will oppose it. Britain will not have it. The post-war international order will not permit it.

"It is impossible to harness the centrifugal forces like those for which Pakistan stands by mere good intentions and friendly treaties. Communities distrustful of each other only learn to work together for common ends if they are disciplined within the established framework of power. In our detestations of the British rule we ignore this truth to which every page of history testifies. We had ministries; we flung them away. We had the certainty of federal unity under the Act of 1935; we spurned it. We had the Cripps' Offer to fight our way to higher international status shoulder; we laughed at it. How can a compromise, however, friendly, with no sanction to enforce it, achieve that unity of aim and effort which the formula seeks to establish?

"After Mr. Jinnah's rejection of the Rajaji Formula, I was not prepared for Gandhiji's effort to arrive at a fresh basis for settlement.... By one stroke nationalism has surrendered to arrogant Disruptionism which had frustrated the destiny of the country. The two-nation theory has now been accepted and brought into operation by Gandhiji. Whatever the verbal jugglery, the Hindu and the Muslim nations are now going to meet in the persons of their most prominent representatives, a consummation which Mr. Jinnah devoutly wished.

"Rajaji Formula being rejected, Gandhiji must concede more to secure even a semblance of a settlement. Two Sovereign States we are never going to have. Independence is still a slogan. Dominion Status which time and again was within easy reach has receded into distance. And in the meantime it is proposed to pledge the country to a futile truce which will perhaps be the beginning of a civil war. (*Pilgrimage to Freedom,* K.M. Munshi, pp. 435-36)

Gandhiji advised Munshi to wait till his talks with Jinnah were over. Munshi assured Gandhiji through his letter of 20 August 1944: "Following your advice, I am not doing anything for the present. I shall see you and decide my course of action after your interview with Jinnah."

The Sikh leaders, Sardar Santok Singh, Sardar Harnam Singh, and Sardar Joginder Singh, issued a joint statement on 14 July 1944 declaring: "We strongly protest against this for and on behalf of the Sikh community and hereby declare that the Sikhs will fight to the bitter end against the proposals." Even Dr. N.B. Khare, Member of the Viceroy's Executive Council, condemned the proposals. V.D. Savarkar, President of Hindu Mahasabha, in a telegram on 20 July 1944 issued from Bombay, criticised Gandhiji and Rajaji for conceding the idea of Pakistan without consulting the other political parties in India, particularly, the Hindu Mahasabha. Savarkar also asked the Bengal Hindu Mahasabha to observe the first week of August as 'Akhand Hindustan Week' or 'the Anti-Pakistan Week'. However, the leaders of the National Federation of India, the National Christian Party of Bombay and even Dr. Ambedkar, who was then a Member of the Viceroy's Executive Council, liked these proposals as an augury for the formation of a national government. Jinnah himself in his address to the half-yearly session of the Muslim League on 30 July 1944, condemned Rajaji formula as a parody, a negation of and an attempt to torpedo the Muslim League's resolution of March 1940. However, he wanted Gandhiji to start personal negotiations with him and declare that this formula showed that Gandhiji in his personal capacity had accepted the principle of the division of India.

The All Party Sikhs' Conference assembled in Amritsar on 1 August 1944 under the presidentship of Sardar Baldev Singh, who was the Development Minister in the Viceroy's Executive Council. It declared unanimously that the basis of communal settlement as proposed in Rajaji's formula and apparently approved by Gandhiji was manifestly unfair and detrimental to the best interests of the country and the Sikh community. Baldev Singh denounced the proposed scheme as breach of faith on the part of the Congress leaders who had assured the Sikhs in their Lahore Session of 1929 that no communal settlement would be acceptable to the Congress which did not satisfy *inter alia* the Sikh community. Once again, on 20 August 1944, under the leadership of Master Tara Singh, the Sikh leaders condemned the Gandhi-Rajaji formula and rejected it saying that, as a result of this, the Sikhs would be divided into sections to be held in perpetual bondage. Thus, the Sikhs in a downright manner rejected the Rajaji formula.

Master Tara Singh criticised Gandhiji saying that he had gone back on his assurance to the Sikhs, and declared that the Sikhs would carry on the agitation until such time as the scheme was dropped.

Master Tara Singh urged Gandhiji to ensure that Sikh interests were not sacrificed at the alter of a Hindu-Muslim pact. To him Gandhiji's response was: "We shall come to no final terms. The smallest interest will have the same weight as the largest."

The Hindu Mahasabha, under the leadership of Dr. Shyama Prasad Mookerjee, rejected the formula and conveyed their feelings to Gandhiji on 5 August 1944.

Rajagopalachari, who had been striving since 1943 to come to an understanding with Jinnah but had been rebuffed by him, once again came forward. He wanted to win over the Liberal leaders, Tej Bahadur Sapru and Jayakar, to his line of thinking. Sapru, when told by Rajaji that he wanted to hold discussions with Jinnah, tried to dissuade him saying that Jinnah would pointblank ask Rajaji, 'Have you any goods to deliver? Whom do you represent? Can you bring the Hindu Mahasabha to any conclusion? Can you come to an understanding on behalf of the Congress?' The Liberals, thus, did not agree with Rajaji's views on Pakistan.

On 13 August 1944, Srinivasa Sastri of the National Liberation Federation, after critically analysing the Rajaji formula, rejected it saying: "I dread this division of India, I dread it like poison." Rajaji's formula, thus, though it was tentatively accepted by Gandhiji, was opposed by the Muslim League, the Hindu Mahasabha, the All Parties Sikh' Conference, including Akali Dal, the Sikh Communist Conference, the All Parties Hindu Conference and the National Liberation Front. Commenting on this Copley comments: "In many respects Gandhi had even greater occasion to regret his friendship with Rajaji during 1944 than 1940. C.R. acted throughout as if he had a mandate from Gandhiji. The evidence, however, suggests that though Gandhiji had agreed to Rajaji's formula as early as March 1943, when they met during Gandhiji's fast, it is hard to resist the conclusion that C.R. took advantage of Gandhi in a moment of weakness." (*A Centenary History of the Indian National Congress*, B.N. Pande, pp. 616-17)

Savarkar asserted that the Indian provinces were not the private properties of Gandhiji and Rajagopalachari, so that they could make a gift of them to anyone they liked.

4

Date-wise Gandhi-Jinnah Talks

In spite of the opinions on the Rajaji Formula Gandhiji remained firm on having talks with Jinnah. The reasons, which prompted Gandhiji to renew the Rajaji offer of Pakistan to Jinnah are given by Pyarelal in *Last Phase,* Vol. I, p. 99:

'How could Gandhiji give his approval to the Rajaji Formula and how dared he concede the principle of Pakistan? Had he not called the partition proposal as untruth and India's vivisection a sin?' Some critics asked. Gandhiji explained that what he had agreed to was not different from the self-determination principle to which the Congress Working Committee was committed. It implied conceding the right to separate such areas as might want it, after ascertaining the wishes of the inhabitants of that area through a properly conducted plebiscite, consistently with the safety, integrity and economic progress of the country as a whole.

'The Rajaji Formula conceded the essence of the League's demand, in so far as it was reasonable,' said Gandhiji. He did not mind if it was given the name of Pakistan.

"If the object was to create a unit where there would be the fullest scope for the development of Muslim religion and culture for the expression of the talents and personality of leaders of the Muslim community, without being overshadowed by more outstanding talent which they feared in undivided India, his formula would give full satisfaction.

"He had the highest regard for Jinnah's single-mindedness, his great ability and integrity which nothing could buy. Surely, Jinnah the patriot would not insist on freedom to engage in a fratricidal war. That is why he had knocked at his door, presented his cards to him for examination and entreated him to produce his without any mental reservation."

A large number of Khaksars – a para-military Muslim organisation in imitation to Hitler's S.S. Organisation based on a Fuehrer principle—had swarmed into Bombay and were holding parades to create the proper atmosphere to stimulate the Congress-League settlement. The Communists were holding mass meetings which would compel the two leaders to unite in the defence of democracy as symbolised by Russian Resistance to Nazi aggression.

The Bombay Police authorities, by way of precaution promulgated an order prohibiting the use of a certain number of roads and public places except by those persons who are resident in the locality surrounding those roads and by persons who genuinely need to visit those persons. To it Jinnah added a characteristic announcement of his own: "Press representatives, I hope, will understand that obviously the meeting is not open to the press and, therefore, I would request them not to take the trouble of coming to my house. Photographers and film companies are at liberty to take photos and shots on the arrival of Mr. Gandhi."

"On the first day of the talk that Gandhi and Jinnah met, they shook hands, they embraced each other. There seemed to be a genuine touch in their first meeting. Jinnah came out in his porch to receive the Mahatma and to escort him back at the time of leaving, and even posed with him to be photographed. Observers fancied they noticed in Jinnah's parting warm handshake more than a mere histrionic gesture." (*Last Phase,* Vol. 1, Pyarelal, pp. 83-84)

The talks commenced on 9 September and ended on 27 September 1944. During this period, Gandhiji walked fourteen times to talk with Jinnah in the latter's house on Mount Pleasant road of Bombay's Malabar Hill. It was a short walk, for Gandhiji too was staying on Mount Pleasant road in Birla House. A letter Gandhiji wrote to Meera speaks of the family and the team supporting him during the exercise, which ultimately proved exercise in futility.

The details of the date-wise talks as given in Vol.77 & 78 of the *Collected Works of Mahatma Gandhi* are reproduced below:

9.9.1944

The meeting lasted three and a quarter hours. Gandhiji reported the talk to Rajagopalchari:

"It was a test of my patience.... I am amazed at my own patience. However, it was a friendly talk. His (Jinnah's) contempt for your formula (Rajaji Formula) and his contempt for you is staggering. You rose in my estimation that you could have talked to him for all those hours and that you should have taken the trouble to draw up that formula.

He says you have accepted his demand and so should I. I said: "I endorse Rajaji's Formula and you can call it Pakistan if you like." He talked of the Lahore Resolution.

I said: "I have not studied it and I do not want to talk about it. Let us talk about Rajaji Formula and you can point out any flaws that you find there."

In the middle of talk, he came to the old ghost: "I thought you had come here as a Hindu, as a representative of the Hindu Congress." I said: No, I have come here neither as a Hindu nor as a representative of the Congress. I have come here as an individual. You can talk to me as an individual or as the President of the League, whichever way you prefer. If you had agreed with Rajaji and accepted his Formula, you and he would have gone before your respective organisations and pleaded with them to accept it. That is why Rajaji came to you. You would have then placed it before other parties, too, in the same way. Now you and I have to do it."

He said that he was the President of the League. Where was the basis for a talk if I was there representing nobody except myself? Who was to deliver the goods? I was the same man as he had found me in 1939. There was no change in me. I almost felt like saying, 'Yes, I am the same man and since you think that it is no use talking to me, I will go away.' But I resisted the temptation.

I told him, "Is it not worth your while to convert an individual? I am the same man no doubt. You can change my views if you can and I will support you wholeheartedly."

"Yes, I know, if I can convert you, you will be my Ali," he said. (Gandhiji observed afterwards: It was a most revealing remark. I was meeting the prophet of Pakistan looking for his Ali.)

He said I should concede Pakistan and he will go the whole length with me. He would go to jail, he would even face bullets.

I said, "I will stand by your side to face them."

"You may not," he said.

"Try me," I replied.

We came back to the formula. He wants Pakistan now not after independence." We will have independence for Pakistan and Hindustan," he said.

We should come to an agreement and then go to the Government and ask them to accept it, force them to accept our solution."

I said, "I could never be a party to that. I could never ask the Britishers to impose Partition on India. If you all want to separate, I cannot stop you. I have not got the power to compel you and I would not use it if I had."

He said "The Muslims want Pakistan. The League represents the Muslims and it wants separation."

I said, "I agree that the League is the most powerful Muslim organisation. I might even concede that you as its president represent the Muslims of India, but that does not mean that all Muslims want Pakistan. Put it to the vote of all inhabitants of the area and see."

He said, "Why should you ask non-Muslims?"

I said, You cannot possibly deprive a section of the population of its vote. You must carry them with you, and if you are in the majority why should you be afraid?"

I told him of what Kiron Shankar Roy had said to me: "If the worst comes to the worst, we in Bengal will all go to Pakistan, but for goodness sake do not partition Bengal. Do not vivisect it."

"If you are in majority," I said, "you will have your choice. I know it is a bad thing for you, but if you want it all the same you will have it. But that will be an adjustment between you and me. It cannot occur while the British are here."

He began to cross-examine me on the various clauses of the Formula. I said to him, "If you want clarification of those things, is it not better to have it from the author of the Formula?

"Oh, no," he did not want that.

I said, "What is the use of cross-examining me?"

He recollected himself. "Oh, no. I am not cross-examining you", and then added: "I have been a lawyer all my life and my manner may have suggested that I was cross-examining you."

I asked him to reduce to writing his objections to the Formula. He was disinclined. "Must I do so?" he asked.

"Yes, I would like you to do." He agreed.

In the end he said, "I would like to come to an agreement with you."

I answered, "You remember what I have said that we should meet not to separate till we had come to an agreement."

He said, "Yes, he agreed."

I suggested, "Should we put that also in our statement?"

He said, "No, better not." Nevertheless that will be an understanding between us and the cordiality and friendliness of our talk will be reflected in our public utterances, too.

In an interview to the press, Jinnah said: "We have had frank and friendly talks and we are resuming our talks on Monday at 5.30 p.m. Tomorrow is the 21 day of Ramzan and therefore, all Musalmans have to observe it. And I have, therefore, requested Mr. Gandhi to oblige me not to have a meeting on the 21 day of Ramza."

A former colleague of Jinnah remarked: "Why did he not say it was Sunday and he wanted a holiday? He understands Sunday better than Ramzan."

"No obliging; willing to surrender." Replied Gandhiji.

At the end of the first day's talks, Jinnah on behalf of Gandhiji and himself, dictated the statement. Earlier, in reply to a question by a newsman whether he had brought anything from Jinnah.

"Only flowers," was the Mahatma's laconic reply.

After Gandhiji gave his report to Rajaji, the following conversation took place between them:

Rajaji: Do you think that he wants a settlement?

Gandhiji: I am not certain. He thought he probably did.

Rajaji: Then you will get it through.

Gandhiji: Yes. If the right word comes to me.

10.9.1944

Following the talks of 9 September, Jinnah sent a letter to Gandhij on 10 September in which he said:

"With reference to our talk yesterday, September 9, I understood from you that you had come to discuss the Hindu-Muslim settlement with me in your individual capacity, and not in any representative character or capacity on behalf of the Hindus or the Congress, nor had you any authority to do so. I naturally pointed out to you that there must be someone on the other side with authority holding a representative status with whom I can negotiate and, if possible, come to a settlement of the Hindu-Muslim question, and that for the position you had adopted there was no precedent, and that this raises great difficulties in my way. As you know, I can only speak on behalf of Muslim India and the All-India Muslim League, as the President of the organisation, which I represent and as such I am subject to and governed by its constitution, rules and regulations I think you realise and will admit that the settlement of the Hindu-Muslim question is a foremost and is a major hurdle, and unless the representatives of these two nations put their heads together, how is one to make any headway with it?"

"Nevertheless, I explained to you the Lahore Resolution of March 1940, and tried to persuade you to accept the basic and fundamental principles embodied in that resolution, but you not only refused to consider it but emphasized your opposition to the basic position indicated in the resolution, and remarked that there was 'an ocean between you and me', and when I asked you what is then the alternative you suggest, you put forward a formula of Mr. Rajagopalachari, approved of by you.

"We discussed it, and as the various matters were vague and nebulous, and some required clarification, I wanted to have a clear idea of what it really meant, and what were its implications, and asked you for explanation and clarification regarding the proposals embodied in the Formula. After some discussion, you requested me to formulate in writing my points that I thought required or called for explanation and clarification, and to communicate with you and that you would reply in writing before our next meeting on Monday September 11 at 5.30 p.m. I am, therefore, submitting to you the following points which required clarification:

"1. With regard to the Preamble: In what capacity will you be a consenting party, if any agreement is reached between you and me?

"2. *Clause 1:* With regard to the Constitution for free India referred to in this clause, I would like to know first, what constitution do you refer to, who will frame it, and when will it come into being?

"Next, it is stated in the Formula that 'the Muslim League endorse the Indian demand for independence.' Does it mean the Congress demand for independence as formulated in the August resolution of 1942 by the All-India Congress Committee in Bombay or, if not, what is the significance of this term, for you know the Muslim League has made it clear not only by its resolution but by its creed, which is embodied in its constitution, that we stand for the freedom and independence of the whole of this subcontinent, and that applies to Pakistan and Hindustan.

"Next, it is stated that the Muslim League will co-operate with the Congress in the formulation of a Provisional Interim Government for the transitional period. I would like to know the basis or the lines on which such a Government is to be set up or constituted. If you have a complete and definite scheme, please let me have it.

"3. *Clause 2:* Who will appoint the Commission referred to in this Clause and who will give effect to their findings? What is the meaning of 'absolute majority' referred to in it? Will the contemplated plebiscite be taken district-wise, or, if not, on what basis? Who will determine and decide whether such a plebiscite should be based on adult franchise or other practicable franchise? Who will give effect to the decision or verdict of the above mentioned plebiscite? Would only the districts on the border which are taken out from the boundaries of the present provinces by delimitation be entitled to choose to join either State or also those out side the present boundaries would have the right to choose to join either state?

"4. *Clause 3:* Who are meant by 'all parties' in this clause?

"5. *Clause 4:* I would like to know between whom and through what machinery and agency will the 'mutual agreements' referred to in this clause be entered into? What is meant by 'safeguarding defence and commerce, and for other essential purposes'? Safeguarding against whom?

6. *Clause 6:* 'These terms shall be binding only in case of transfer by Britain of full power and responsibility for the Government of India.' I would like to know to whom is this power to be transferred, through what machinery and agency, and when?

"These are some of the important points that occur to me for the moment, which require explanation and clarification, and hope that you will let me have full details with regard to the various points that I have raised, in order that I may be better able to understand and judge your proposals before I can deal with them satisfactorily."

11.9.1944

Gandhiji sent the clarification to Jinnah vide his letter dated September 11, as follows: "I received your letter yesterday at 3.30 p.m. I was in the midst of appointments. I hasten to reply at the earliest opportunity."

"I have said it in my letter to you, it is implied in the Rajaji Formula and I have stated publicly that I have approached you as an individual. My life mission has been Hindu-Muslim unity which I want for its sake, but which is not to be achieved without the foreign ruling power being ousted. Hence the first condition of the exercise of the right of self-determination is achieving independence by the joint action of all the parties and groups composing India. If such joint action is unfortunately impossible, then too I must fight with the assistance of such elements as can be brought together. I am glad, therefore, that you did not break off our talks when I refused to assume or accept a representative capacity. I am pledged to use all the influence I may have with the congress to ratify my agreement with you. May I remind you that the Rajaji Formula was designed in the first instance for your acceptance, and submission thereafter to the League?

"It is true that I said an ocean separated you and me in outlook. But that had no reference to the Lahore Resolution of the League. The Lahore Resolution is indefinite. Rajaji has taken from it the substance and given it a shape.

"Now for the points raised by you:

"1. I have already answered this in the foregoing.

"2. The constitution will be framed by the Provisional Government contemplated in the Formula or an authority specially set up by it after the British power is withdrawn. The independence contemplated is of the whole India as it stands.

"The basis for the formation of Provisional Interim Government will have to be agreed to between the League and the Congress.

"3. The Commission will be appointed by the Provisional Government. 'Absolute majority' means a clear majority over non-Muslim elements as in Sind, Baluchistan or the Frontier Province. The Form of plebiscite and franchise must be a matter for discussion.

"4. 'All parties' means, the parties interested.

"5. 'Mutual agreement' means agreement between contracting parties. 'Safeguarding defence etc.,' means for me a central or joint board of control. Safeguard means safeguarding against all who may put the common interests in jeopardy.

"6. The power is to be transferred to the nation, that is, to the Provisional Government. The Formula contemplates peaceful transfer by the British Government. So far as I am concerned, I would like the transfer to take place as early as possible."

The talks were resumed in the evening on the 11 September. The Mahatma had his evening meal in the middle of their conversation at Jinnah's residence. A bottle of boiled water was included in his tiffin basket. Lest anyone should think that the Mahatma was using holy Ganges water or something like that when dining in a Muslim house, Gandhiji gave instructions that the water bottle was not to be sent along thereafter anymore.

Gandhiji's Speech at Prayer Meeting on 11.9.1944

Gandhiji made a speech at a prayer meeting in Bombay in the evening of September 11. Referring to his meeting with Jinnah he said:

"He knew how eager they must be to be acquainted with the progress of the talks. It was a natural eagerness on their part which he would like to satisfy as far as possible consistently with the interest of the cause which they all shared with him in common."

All that he could say at the present stage was that Jinnah Saheb and he had met as old friends on Saturday (September 9), and again that day (Monday). He added that they would be meeting again the next day from 10.30 a.m. to 1 p.m. and from 5.30 to 7 p.m. This would leave them a little time to attend to other work and to digest the substance of the talks. They fully realised what a heavy responsibility rested on their shoulders; they know that the millions were watching the talks and were anxious that a settlement should be arrived at which would subserve the interests not of any particular group or community, but of the whole of India.

"Our goal is the attainment of independence for the whole of India. It is for that we pray and are pledged to lay down our lives. Jinnah Saheb and I have only God between us as witness. My constant prayer these days is that He may so guide my speech that not a word might escape my lips so as to hurt the feelings of Jinnah Saheb or damage the cause so dear to us both. He told me today, 'If we part without coming to an agreement, we shall proclaim bankruptcy of wisdom on our part.' What is more, the hopes of millions of our countrymen will be dashed to pieces. Today, the eyes of all the oppressed people of the world are on us. We therefore are fully alive to our responsibility and are straining every nerve to come to a settlement. But, we realise that ultimately the result lies in God's good hands. You should therefore all pray that He may guide us and give us wisdom to serve the cause of India."

In conclusion Gandhiji appealed to the press to put a curb on their inventiveness and not to give free rein to their imagination. Since neither he nor Mr. Jinnah was opening his lips to anybody, there could be no question of leakage.

Gandhiji gave an assurance that he would not sacrifice the interest of a single individual or community.

11.9.1944

Jinnah wrote a letter to Gandhiji on September 11, in which he said:

"I note that you have approached me as an individual, and I have already expressed my views about it. Nevertheless, I proceeded to discuss matters with you because I am anxious to convert you to my point of view, if possible. I urged you that the only solution of India's problem is to accept the division of India as Pakistan and Hindustan, as briefly laid down in Lahore Resolution of March 1940, and proceed to settle the details forthwith.

"1. You say that Lahore Resolution is indefinite. You never asked me for any clarification or explanation of the terms of the Resolution, but you really indicated your emphatic opposition to the very basis and the fundamental principles embodied in it. I would, therefore, like to know in what way or respect the Lahore Resolution is indefinite. I cannot agree that Rajaji has taken from it its substance and given it shape but mutilated it, as I explained in my speech which I delivered at the meeting of the Council of the All-India Muslim League at Lahore on the 30 July, 1944.

"2. You say that the first condition of the exercise of the right of self-determination is achieving independence by the joint action of all the parties and groups composing India. If such joint action is unfortunately impossible, then, too, I must fight with the assistance of such elements as can be brought together. This in my opinion is, I have repeatedly said, putting the cart before the horse, and is generally opposed to the policy and declaration of the All-India Muslim League, and you are only holding on firmly to the August Resolution of 1942. In order to achieve the freedom and independence of the peoples of India, it is essential, in the first instance, that there should be a Hindu-Muslim settlement. Of course, I am thankful to you when you say that you are pledged to use all the influence that you have with the Congress to ratify your agreement with me, but that is not enough in my judgment, although it will be a very valuable help to me. I once more ask you, please, to let me know what is your conception of the basis for the formation of a Provisional Interim Government. No doubt it will be subject to agreement between the League and the Congress, but I think in fairness you should at least give me some rough idea of the lines of your conception, for you must have thought it out by now, and I would like to know what are your proposals or scheme for the formation of a Provisional Interim Government, which can give me some clear picture to understand.

"3. You have omitted to answer my question as to who will give effect to the findings of the Commission, and also it is not clear to me what you mean by absolute majority, when you say it means 'a clear majority over non-Muslim elements as in Sind, Baluchistan or Frontier Province'. You have not even replied to my question as to who will decide the form of the plebiscite and the franchise contemplated by the Formula.

"4. The answer does not carry any clear idea when you say 'all parties means parties interested'.

"5. You say 'mutual agreement means agreement between contracting parties,' who are the contracting parties once a Provisional Interim Government is established of your conception? Who will appoint the Central or Joint Board of Control, which will safeguard defence, etc., and on what machinery and agency, and subject to whose control and orders will such Central or Joint Board be?

"6. You say, 'the power is to be transferred to the nation that is, to Provisional Government'. That is all the greater reason why I would like to know full details of the Provisional Government as contemplated by you and of your conception."

12.9.1944

Gandhiji reported his talk which he had with Jinnah on 12 September to Rajaji:

Jinnah drew a very alluring picture of the Government of Pakistan. It would be a perfect democracy. I asked him if he had not told me that democracy did not suit Indian conditions. He did not remember it. He asked me to tell him what he had said. So I told him all that and said that I might have misunderstood him. In that case he should correct me. But when I repeated in detail what he had said, he could not say no. He said, yes, he had said that, but that was with regard to imposed democracy.

Then he said, "Do you think it is a question of religious minority with us?"

I said, "yes."

If not, he should tell me what it was. He harangued. I won't repeat all that here. I asked him what would happen to the other minorities in Pakistan: Sikhs, Christians, Depressed classes, etc. He said they would be part of Pakistan. I asked him if he meant joint electorates. He knew I was coming to it. He said, yes, he would like them to be a part of the whole. He would explain the advantages of joint electorates, but if they wanted separate electorates they would have it. Sikhs would have Gurmukhi if they wanted and the Pakistan Government would give them financial aid.

I asked, "What about Jats?"

At first he pooh-poohed the idea. Then he said, "If they want it, they will also have it. They will have separate existence if they want it."

I said, "What about Christians? They also want some place where they are in a majority and where they can rule, as for instance in Travancore?"

He said that was a problem for the Hindus.

I said, "supposing Travancore was in Pakistan?" He said he would give it to them. He cited the instance of Newfoundland.

The rest of the talk was nothing. I am to continue exploring his mind.

Dialogue with Rajaji

Gandhiji had the following dialogue with Rajaji on September 12, 1944.

Rajaji: Find out what Jinnah wants?

Gandhiji: Yes, that is what I am trying. I want to prove from his own mouth that the whole of the Pakistan proposition is absurd. I think he does not want to break. On my part I am not going to be in a hurry. But he cannot expect me to endorse an undefined Pakistan.

Rajaji: Do you think he will give up the claim?

Gandhiji: He has to, if there is to be a settlement. He wants a settlement, but what he wants he does not know. I want to show him that your Formula is the only thing that he can reasonably ask for. (*Collected Works of Mahatma Gandhi,* Vol. 78, pp. 87)

13.9.1944 Interview to Press

After the morning session of the talks, as Gandhiji and Jinnah emerged, the waiting group of reporters asked: "Anything for us?" The leaders halted and Gandhiji spoke: "I have nothing but I will go for you. Yesterday you read something in our faces. Here are we both. I would like you not to read anything in our faces except hope and nothing but hope."

Gandhiji turned to Jinnah and asked: "Am I right? Have you seen the papers this morning?"

"Why bother?" answered Jinnah. "They have written so much terrible."

Gandhiji turned round to the press again and said, "You do not know what people who are bent on mischief will do. All of you know both of us. You should leave us absolutely alone, or if you can read our hearts and faces you must submit what you have written to one of us. Otherwise you should be absolutely silent if you want to serve India and humanity."

14.9.1944

In his letter of September 14 Gandhiji wrote to Jinnah:

"I have your letter of the 13 instant. I understand from our talks that you were in no hurry for my answer. I was, therefore, taking the matter in a leisurely fashion, even hoping that as our talks proceeded and as cordiality increased, mutual clarification would come of itself and that we would only have to record our final agreement. But I understand and appreciate the other viewpoint. We should take nothing for granted. I should clarify your difficulties in understanding the Rajaji Formula and you should do likewise regarding yours, i.e., the Muslim League Lahore Resolution of 1940.

"With reference to the Lahore resolution, as agreed between us I shall deal with it in a separate letter.

"Perhaps at the end of our discussions, we shall discover that Rajaji not only has not put the Lahore Resolution out of shape and mutilated it but has given it substance and form.

"Indeed, in view of your dislike for the Rajaji Formula, I have, put it out of my mind and I am concentrating on the Lahore Resolution in the hope of finding a ground of mutual agreement.

"So much for the first paragraph of your letter.

"As the second, I do hold that unless we oust the third party we shall not be able to leave at peace with one another. That does not mean that I may not make an effort to find ways and means of establishing a living peace between us.

"You ask for my conception of the basis for a Provisional Interim Government. I would have told you if I had any scheme in mind. I imagine that if we two can agree it would be for us to consult the other parties. I can say this that any provisional government to inspire confidence at the present moment must represent all parties. When that moment arrives, I shall have been replaced by some authoritative person, though you will have me always at your beck and call when you have converted me or I you, or by mutual conversion we have become one mind functioning through two bodies.

"As the third point the provisional Government, being the appointing authority, will give effect to the findings of the Commission. This I thought was implied in my previous answer.

"Rajaji tells me 'absolute majority' is used in his Formula in the same sense as it is used in ordinary legal parlance wherever more than two groups are dealt with. I cling to my own answer. But you will perhaps suggest a third meaning and persuade me to accept it.

"The form of the plebiscite and franchise must be left to be decided by the provisional interim government unless we decide it now. I should say it should be by adult suffrage of all the inhabitants of the Pakistan area.

"As to the fourth, all parties means you and I and everyone else holding views on the question at issue will and should seek by peaceful persuasion to influence public opinion as is done where democracy functions wholly or in part.

"As to the fifth, supposing that the result of the plebiscite is in favor of partition, the provisional government will draft the treaty and agreements as regards the administration of matters of common interest, but the same has to be confirmed and ratified by the governments of the two States. The machinery required for the settlement and administration of matters of common interest will, in the first instance, be planned by the Interim Government, but subsequently will be matter of the settlement between the two governments acting through the agencies appointed by each for that purpose.

"As to the sixth, I hope the foregoing makes superfluous any further reply."

14.9.1944

Jinnah sent his reply on September 14 to Gandhiji as follows:

"1. Please let me have as soon as you can your promised letter indicating in what way or respect the Lahore Resolution is 'indefinite.'

"2. With regard to the provision in the Gandhi-Rajaji Formula that 'the Muslim League endorses the Indian demand for independence,' I asked you in my letter of September 10, 'Does it mean the Congress demand for independence, as formulated in the August 1942 resolution by the All India Congress Committee in Bombay or, if not, what is the significance of this term?', to which you replied by your letter of September 11. 'The independence contemplated is of the whole of India as it stands.' Hence I again ask, does it mean on the basis of a United India? I find that you have not clarified the point satisfactorily.

"3. As regards the next part of the clause, the Formula proceeds to lay down that 'the Muslim League will cooperate with the Congress in the formation of the Provisional Interim Government for the transitional period.' I requested you by my letter of September 10, to let me know the basis or the lines on which such a government is to be set up or constituted. If you have a complete and definite scheme, please let me know, to which you replied that the basis for the formation of the Provisional Interim Government will have to be agreed to between the League and the Congress. But that is not meeting my request for clarification, or giving me at least the outline of such a government. And that is what I have been asking for. I hope that you do appreciate my point when I am requesting you to let me have rough outlines of the proposed Provisional Interim Government according to the Formula, so that I may have some idea. Of course, I can quite understand that such a Provisional Interim Government will represent all the parties and would be of a character that will inspire confidence at the present moment of all the parties. I can quite understand that when the moment arrives, certain things may follow but before we can deal with this Formula in a satisfactory manner, I repeat again that as it is your Formula, you should give me a rough idea of the Provisional Interim Government that you contemplated and of your conception. What I would like to know would be what will be the powers of such a government, how it will be formed, to whom it will be responsible, and what will be its composition, etc. You, being the sponsor of this Gandhi-Rajaji Formula, should give me some rough idea and picture of it, so that I may understand what this part of the Formula means.

"4. In your letter of September 14, in reply to my letter of September 11, you inform me that you would have told me if you had any scheme in mind. I imagine that if we two can agree it would be for us to consult the other parties. Unless I have some outlines or scheme, from you, what are we to discuss in order to reach any agreement?

"5. As regards the other matters which you have further explained, I have noted the explanation, and I do not think I need press you further, although some of them are not quite satisfactory."

15.9.1944

Gandhiji's letter of September 15 to Jinnah says:

"This is in terms of our talks of Wednesday the 13 instant.

'For the moment I have shunted the Rajaji Formula and with your assistance I am applying my mind very seriously to the famous Lahore Resolution of the Muslim League.'

"You must admit that the resolution itself makes no reference to the two-nation theory. In the course of our discussions, you have passionately pleaded that India contains two nations, i.e., Hindus and Muslims, and the later have their homelands in India as the former have theirs. The more our argument progresses, the more alarming your picture appears to me. It would be alluring if it was true. But my fear is growing that it is wholly unreal. I find no parallel in history for a body of converts and their descendents claiming to be a nation apart from the parent stock. If India was one nation before the advent of Islam, it must remain one in spite of the change of faith of a very large body of her children.

"You do not claim to be a separate nation by right of conquest, but by reason of acceptance of Islam. Will the two nations become one if the whole India accepted Islam? Will Bengalis, Oriyas, Andhras, Tamilians, Maharashtrians, Gujaratis, etc., cease to have their special characteristics if all of them become converts to Islam? These have all become one politically because they are subject to one foreign control. They are trying today to throw off that subjection.

"You seem to have introduced a new test of nationhood. If I accept it, I would have to subscribe to many more claims and face an insoluble problem. The only real, though awful, test of our nationhood arises out of our common political subjection. If you and I throw off this subjection by our combined effort, we shall be a politically free nation out of our travail. If by then we have not learnt to prize our freedom, we may quarrel among ourselves and, for want of common master holding us together in his iron grip, seek to split up into small groups or nationalities. There will be nothing to prevent us from descending to that level and we shall not have to go in search of a master. There are many claimants to the throne that never remains vacant.

"With this background, I shall present you with my difficulty in accepting your Resolution.

"1. Pakistan is not in the Resolution. Does it bear the original meaning Punjab, Afghanistan, Kashmir, Sind, and Baluchistan, out of which the name was mnemonically formed? If not what is it?

"2. Is the goal of Pakistan Pan-Islam?

"3. What is it that distinguishes an Indian Muslim from every other Indian, if not his religion? Is he different from a Turk or an Arab?

"4. What is the connotation of the word 'Muslims' in the Resolution under discussion? Does it mean the Muslims of India of geography or the Pakistan to be?

"5. Is the Resolution addressed to the Muslims by way of education, or to the inhabitants of the whole of India by way of appeal, or to the foreign ruler as an ultimatum?

"6. Are the constituents in the two zones to constitute 'Independent States', as undefined number in each zone?

"7. Is the demarcation to take place during the tendency of British Rule?

"8. If the answer to the last question is in affirmative, the proposal must be accepted first by Britain and then imposed upon India, not evolved from within by the free will of the people of India.

"9. Have you examined the position and satisfied yourself that these 'Independent States' will be materially and otherwise benefited by being split up into fragments?

"10. Please satisfy me that these Independent Sovereign States will not become a collection of poor States, a menace to themselves and to the rest of India.

"11. Pray show me by facts and figures or otherwise how the independence and welfare of India as a whole can be brought about by the acceptance of the resolution.

"12. How are the Muslims under the Princes to be disposed of as a result of this scheme?

"13. What is your definition of 'minorities'?

"14. Will you please define the 'adequate, effective and mandatory safeguards' for minorities referred to in the second part of the Resolution?

"15. Do you not see that the Lahore Resolution contains only a bare statement of the objective and does not give any idea as to the means to be adopted for the execution of the idea and the concrete corollaries thereof? For instance: (a) Are the people in the regions falling under the plan to have any voice in the matter of separation and, if so, how is it to be ascertained? (b) What is the provision for the defence and similar matters of common concern contemplated in the Lahore Resolution? (c) There are many groups of Muslims who have continuously expressed dissent from the policy of the League.

> While I am prepared to accept the preponderating influence and position of the League and have approached you for that very reason, is it not our joint duty to remove their doubts and carry them with us? By making them feel that they and their supporters have not been practically disfranchised.
> (d) Does this not lead again to placing the Resolution of the League before the people of the zones concerned as a whole for acceptance?

"As I write this letter and imagine the working of the resolution in practice, I see nothing but ruin for the whole of India, for I realise in my own person their misery and degradation, which is their common lot, irrespective of class, caste or creed. I know that you have acquired a unique hold on the Muslim masses. I want you to use your influence for their total welfare, which must include the rest.

"In this hastily written letter, I have only given an inkling of my difficulty."

15.9.1944

Gandhiji sent another letter to Jinnah on September 15 in which he said:

"Independence does not mean as envisaged in the A.I.C.C. Resolution of 1942. But it cannot be on the basis of a United India. If we come to a settlement, it would be on the basis of the settlement, assuming, of course, that it accrues general acceptance in the country. The process will be somewhat like this. We reach by joint effort independence for India as it stands. India becoming free will proceed to demarcation, plebiscite and partition if the people concerned vote for partition. All this is implied in the Rajaji Formula.

"As to the provisional Interim Government, I am afraid I cannot carry my answer any further than I have done. Though I have no scheme for the Provisional Government, if you have one in connection with the Lahore Resolution, which also, I presume, requires an Interim Government, we can discuss it.

"The Formula was framed by Rajaji in good faith. I accepted it in equal good faith. The hope was that you would look at it with favour. We still think it would be the best in the circumstances. You and I have to put flesh on it, if we can. I have explained process we have to go through. You have no objection to it. Perhaps, you want to know how I would form the Provisional Government if I was invited thereto. If I was in that unenviable position, I would see all the claimants and endeavour to satisfy them. My cooperation will be available in that task.

"I can give you full satisfaction about your inquiry, 'What I would like to know would be, what will be powers of such a Provisional Interim Government, how it will be formed, to whom it will be responsible.' The Provisional Interim Government will be responsible to the elected members of the present Assembly or a newly elected one. It will have all the powers less that of the Commander-in-Chief during the war and full powers thereafter. It will be the authority to give effect to the agreement that may be arrived at between the League and the Congress and ratified by the other parties."

17.9.1944

Jinnah sent his letter dated September 17 in reply to to Gandhiji's letter of September 15, in which he said:

"I note that you have for the moment shunted the Rajaji Formula and are applying your mind very seriously to the

Lahore Resolution of the Muslim League. It is my duty to explain the Lahore resolution to you today and persuade you to accept it, even though you are talking to me, as you have often made it clear, in your individual capacity. I have successfully converted non-Muslim Indians in no small number and also a larger body of foreigners, and if I can convert you, it will be no small assistance to me although we are not proceeding on the footing that you are carrying on these talks in your representative character or capacity, and my difficulties remain until you are vested with a representative status and authority in order to negotiate and reach an agreement with you.

"You have stated in your letter dated September 11 that the Lahore Resolution is 'indefinite.' I, therefore, naturally asked you to please let me know in what way or respect the Lahore Resolution is indefinite, and now I have received your letter of September 15 under reply.

"The third paragraph of your letter is not seeking clarification, but a disquisition and expression of your views on the point, whether the Musalmans are a nation. This matter can hardly be discussed by means of correspondence. There is a great deal of discussion and literature on this point which is available and it is for you to judge finally, whether the Musalmans and Hindus are not two major nations in this subcontinent. For the moment, I would refer you to two publications, although there are many more – Dr. Ambedkar's book and M.R.T's *Nationalism in Conflict in India*. We maintain and hold that Muslims and Hindus are two major nations by any definition or test of a nation. We are a nation of hundred million, and what is more, we are a nation with our own distinctive culture and civilisation, language and literature, art and architecture, names and nomenclature, sense of value and proportion, legal laws and moral codes, customs and calendar, history and traditions, aptitude and ambitions; in short, we have our own, distinctive outlook on life and of life. By all canons of international law we are a nation. Now I shall reply to your various points:

"1. Yes, the word 'Pakistan' is not mentioned in the Resolution and it does not bear the original meaning. The word has now become synonymous with the Lahore Resolution.

"2. This point does not arise, but still I reply that the question is a mere bogy.

"3. This point is covered by my answer that the Musalmans of India are a nation. As to the last part of your query, it is hardly relevant to the matter of clarification of the Resolution.

"4. Surely, you know what the word 'Muslims' means.

"5. This point does not arise by way of clarification of the test of the Lahore Resolution.

"6. No. They will form units of Pakistan.

"7. As soon as the basis and the principles embodied in the Lahore Resolution are accepted, the question of demarcation will have to be taken up immediately.

"8. In view of my reply to (7), your question (8) has been answered.

"9. Does not relate to clarification.

"10. My answer to (9) covers this point.

"11. Does not arise out of the clarification of the Resolution. Surely, this is not asking for clarification of the Resolution. I have in numerous speeches of mine and the Muslim League in its resolutions have pointed out that this is the only solution of India's problem and the road to achieve freedom and independence of the people of India.

"12. 'Muslims under the princes': The Lahore resolution is only confined to British India. This question does not arise out of clarification of the resolution.

"13. The definition of 'minorities': You yourself have often said minorities mean 'accepted minorities.'

"14. The adequate, effective and mandatory safeguards for minorities referred to in the Resolution are a matter of negotiations and settlement with the minorities in the respective states, viz., Pakistan and Hindustan

"15. It does give basic principles and when they are accepted, then the details will have to be worked out by the contracting parties. (a & b). Does not arise by way of clarification; (c) The Muslim League is the only authoritative and representative organisation of Muslim India; (d) No. See answer (c).

"As regards your final paragraph, before receiving clarification from me you have already passed your judgment and condemned the Lahore Resolution, when you say, 'As I write the letter and imagine the working of the Resolution in practice I see nothing but ruin for the whole of India.' I understand that you have made clear to me that you represent nobody but yourself, and I am trying to persuade you and to convert you that this is the road which will leads us all to the achievement of freedom and independence, not only of the two major nations, Hindus and Musalmans, but the rest of the peoples of India, but when you proceed to say that you aspire to represent all the inhabitants of India, I regret that I cannot accept that statement of yours. It is quite clear that you represent nobody else but the Hindus, and as long as you do not realise your true position and the realities, it is very difficult for me to argue with you, and it becomes still more difficult to persuade you, and hope to convert you to the realities and actual conditions prevailing in India today. I am pleading before you in the hope of converting you, as I have done with many others successfully. As I have said before, You are a great man and you exercise enormous influence over the Hindus, particularly the masses, and by accepting the road that I am pointing out to you, you are not prejudicing or harming the interest of Hindus or of the minorities. On contrary, Hindus will be the great gainers. I am convinced that true welfare not only of the Muslims but the rest of India lies in the division of India as proposed by the Lahore Resolution. It is for you to consider whether it is not your policy and program, in which you have persisted, which has been the principle factor of 'ruin' of the whole of India and of misery and degradation of the people to which you refer and which I deplore no less than anyone else. And it is for that very reason I am pleading before you all these days, although you insist that you are having talks with me only in your individual capacity, in the hope that you may yet revise your policy and program."

18.9.1944

Gandhiji wrote to Meera on 18 September: "My talks are dragging on. God alone knows the end of them. There is one good thing. I am bearing the strain well. I am keeping fit in spite of the two enemies within-the hookworm and the amoeba.

"It is good too that we are within stone's throw of each other. Manilal is attending me. Devadas too is here, so is Rajaji, Khurshedbehn (a granddaughter of Dadabhoy Naoroji) is on the staff and so is Mridula. They are working full speed—not to mention Pyarelal, Sushila and Kanu.

Pyarelal has a shorthand writer and typist. He is a rare man-silent and hardworking.

"Abha is here for medical examination. There is nothing wrong with her. Manu has come back from Karachi with her father. Pyarelal's mother and infant niece, too are here. And they are all very happy." (*Mohandas—A True Story of a Man, His People and an Empire: Rajmohan Gandhi*, pp. 527-28)

19.9.1944

Gandhiji sent his reply to Jinnah through his letter of September 19, in which he said:

"Many thanks for yours 17 instant.

"I am sorry to have to say that your answers omitting 1, 2 and 6 do not give satisfaction.

"It may be that all my questions do not arise from the view of mere clarification of the Lahore Resolution. But I contend that they are very relevant from the standpoint of a seeker and that I am. You cannot expect anyone to agree to or shoulder the burden of the claim contained in the Lahore Resolution without, for instance, answering my questions 15 (a) and 15 (b) which brush aside as not arising by way of clarification.

"Dr. Ambedkar's thesis, while it is ably written, has carried no conviction with me. The other book mentioned by you, I am sorry to say, I have not seen.

"Why can you not accept my statement that I aspire to represent all the sections that compose the people of India? Do you not aspire? Should not every Indian? That the aspiration may never be realised is beside the point.

"I am beholden to you, in spite of your opinion about me, for having patience with me. I hope you will never lose it, but will persevere in your effort to convert me. I ask you to take me with my strong views and even prejudices, if I am guilty of any.

"As to your verdict on my policy and programme, we must agree to differ. For, I am wholly unrepentant. My purpose is as a lover of communal unity to place my services at your disposal.

"I hope you do not expect me to accept the Lahore Resolution without understanding its implications. If your letter is the final word, there is little hope. Can we not agree to differ on the question of 'two nations' and yet solve the problem on the basis of self-determination? It is the basis that has brought me to you. If the regions holding Muslim majorities have to be separated according to the Lahore Resolution, the grave step of separation should be specifically placed before and approved by the people in that area."

21.9.1944

Jinnah in his letter of September 21 to Gandhiji said:

"I am in receipt of your letter of September 19 and I have given you my answers to all your questions relating to clarification of the Lahore Resolution or any part of it, and I am glad that you admit when you say it may be that 'all my questions do not arise from the view of mere clarification of the Lahore Resolution,' you particularly emphasize your points 15 (a) and 15 (b).

"I regret to say that it has no relation to the context of the Resolution or any part thereof. You have brought so many matters into our correspondence, which are entirely outside the matter requiring clarification, so I have perforce to deal with them. Let me first deal with your letter of September 11.

"You say, 'My life mission has been Hindu-Muslim unity, which I want for its own sake but which is not to be achieved without the foreign ruling power being ousted. Hence the first condition of the exercise of the right of self-determination is achieving independence by the joint action of all parties and groups composing India. If such joint action is unfortunately impossible, then too I must fight with the assistance of such elements as can be brought together.'

"The gist of your letters uptodate is that you are wedded to this policy and will pursue it. In your next letter of September 14, while you were good enough to furnish me with the clarification of the Gandhi-Rajaji Formula, you were pleased to observe: 'I have, at any rate for the moment, put it out of my mind and I am now concentrating on the Lahore Resolution in the hope of finding a ground for mutual agreement.' In your letter of September 15, you say, 'Independence does not mean as envisaged in the A.I.C.C Resolution of 1942.' It is, therefore, clear that you are not prepared to revise your policy and that you adhere firmly to your policy and programme, which you have persisted in and which culminated in your demand, final policy, program and the method and sanction for enforcing it by resorting it to mass civil disobedience in terms of the August 8, 1942, Resolution, and you have made it more clear again by stating in your letter of September 19 as follows: 'As to your verdict on my policy and programme, we must agree to differ. For, I am wholly unrepentant.' You know that the August 1942 Resolution is inimical to the ideals and demands of Muslim India. Then again, in the course of our discussion when I asked you for clarification of the Gandhi-Rajaji Formula, you were pleased to say, by your letter of September 15 as follows: 'For the moment I have shunted the Rajaji Formula and with your assistance am applying my mind very seriously to the famous Lahore

Resolution of the Muslim League.' We discussed it in its various aspects, as you told me you were open to be persuaded and converted to our point of view. I discussed the Resolution at great length with you, and explained everything you wanted to understand, even though you have emphasized more than once that you are having these talks with me in your personal capacity, and in your letter of September 15, you assured me in the following words with regard to the Lahore Resolution: 'Believe me, I approach you as a seeker, though I represent nobody but myself,' and that you were open to conviction and conversion. You had informed me by your letter of September 11 as follows: 'It is true that I said an ocean separated you and me in outlook. But that had no reference to the Lahore Resolution of the League. The League Resolution is indefinite.' I naturally, therefore, proceeded in reply to ask you by my letter of September 11 as follows: 'You say the Lahore Resolution is indefinite.' You never asked me for any clarification or the explanation of the terms of the Lahore Resolution, but you really indicated your emphatic opposition to the very basis and the fundamental principles embodied in it. I would, therefore, like to know in what way or respect the Lahore Resolution is indefinite, and I sent you a reminder on September 13, to which you replied by your letter of September 15, not confining yourself really to matters of clarification, but introducing other extraneous matters, with some of which I had already dealt, in reply to this letter of yours of September 15, by my letter of September 17 and furnished you with all the clarification, informing you that you had introduced several matters which could hardly be discussed in a satisfactory manner by means of correspondence. I have already given you all the clarification you require so far as the Lahore Resolution goes and its text is concerned. You again raise further arguments, reasons and grounds and continue to persist in a disquisition on the point, amongst others, whether Muslims of India are a nation, and then you proceed further to say: 'Can we not agree to differ on the question of two nations and yet solve the problem on the basis of self-determination?' It seems to me that you are laboring under some misconception of the real meaning of the word 'self-determination.' Apart from the inconsistencies and contradictions of the various positions that you have adopted in the course of our correspondence, as indicated above, can you not appreciate our point of view that we claim the right of self-determination as a nation and not as a territorial unit, and that we are entitled to exercise our inherent right as a Muslim nation, which is our birth-right? Whereas you are labouring under the wrong idea that 'self-determination' means only that of 'a territorial unit' which, by the way, is neither demarcated nor defined yet; and there is no Union or Federal Constitution of India in being, functioning as a Sovereign Central Government. Ours is a case of division and carving out two independent sovereign States by way of settlement between two major nations, Hindus and Muslims, and not of severance or secession from any existing union, which is non-existent in India. The right of self-determination which we claim postulates that we are a nation, and as such it would be the self-determination of the Musalmans, and they alone are entitled to exercise that right.

"I hope you will now understand that your question 15 (a) does not arise out of the Lahore Resolution or of any part thereof. As to 15 (b), again it does not arise as a matter of clarification, for it will be a matter for the constitution-making body chosen by Pakistan to deal with and decide all matters as a sovereign body representing Pakistan *vis-a-vis* constitution-making body of Hindustan or any other part concerned. There cannot be Defence or similar matters of 'common concern' when it is accepted that Pakistan and Hindustan will be two separate independent sovereign States. I hope I have now given all satisfactory explanations, over and above the matter of clarification of the Lahore Resolution, in the hope of converting you as an individual 'seeker.'

22.9.1944

Gandhiji sent his letter of September 22, to Jinnah in which he said:

"Your letter of yesterday 21 instant so disturbed me that I thought I would postpone my reply till after we had met at the usual time. Though I made no advance at our meeting, I think I see somewhat clearly what you are driving at. The more I think about the two-nation theory the more alarming it appears to be. The book recommended by you gives me no help. It contains self-truths and its conclusions or inferences are unwarranted. I am unable to accept the proposition that the Muslims of India are a nation, distinct from the rest of the inhabitants of India. Mere assertion is no proof. The consequences of accepting such a proposition are dangerous in the extreme. Once the principle is admitted there would be no limit to claims of cutting up India into numerous divisions, which would spell India's ruin. I have, therefore, suggested a way out. Let it be partition as between two brothers, if a division there must be.

"You seem to be averse to a plebiscite. In spite of the admitted importance of the League, there must be clear proof that the people affected desire partition. In my opinion, all the people inhabiting the area ought to express their opinion specifically on this single issue of division.

Adult suffrage is the best method, but I would accept any other equivalent.

"You summarily reject the idea of common interest between the two arms. I can be no willing party to a division which does not provide for the simultaneous safeguarding of common interests, such as, Defence, Foreign Affairs and the like. There will be no feeling of security by the people of India without the recognition of the natural and mutual obligations arising out of a physical contiguity.

"Your letter shows a wide divergence of opinion and outlook between us. Thus you adhere to the opinion often expressed by you that the August 1942 Resolution is 'inimical to the ideals and demands of Muslim India.' There is no proof for this sweeping statement.

"We seem to be moving in a circle. I have made a suggestion. If we are bent on agreeing, as I hope we are, let us call a third party or parties to guide or even arbitrate between us."

23.9.1944

Jinnah sent a letter to Gandhiji on September 23, in which he said:

"I am in receipt of your letter of September 22 and thank you for it. I am sorry that you think I have summarily rejected the idea of common interest between two arms, and now you put it somewhat differently from 15 (a), when you say there will be no feeling of security by the people of India without a recognition of the natural and mutual obligations arising out of physical contiguity. My answer already given is that it will be for the constitution-making body of Pakistan and that of Hindustan, or any other party concerned, to deal with such matters on the footing of their being two independent States.

"I am really surprised when you say there is no proof of what you characterise as a sweeping statement of mine, that the August 1942 Resolution is inimical to the ideals and demands of Muslim India. The Resolution in its essence is as follows:

"a) Immediate grant of Complete Independence (and) setting up immediately of a Federal Central Government on the basis of a united, democratic Government of India with federated units or provinces, which means establishing a Hindu Raj.

"b) That this National Government so set up will evolve a scheme for a Constituent Assembly, which will be chosen by adult franchise, which will prepare a constitution for the Government of India, which means that the Constituent Assembly chosen will be composed of an overwhelming majority of the Hindus, nearly 75 per cent.

"c) To enforce this demand of the Congress the August Resolution decides on and sanctions a resort to mass civil disobedience at your command and when ordered by you as the sole Dictator of the Congress.

"This demand is basically and fundamentally opposed to the ideals and demands of Muslim India of Pakistan, as embodied in the Lahore Resolution, and to enforce such a demand by means of resort to mass civil disobedience is inimical to the ideals and demands of Muslim India, and if you succeed in realising this demand it would be death-blow to Muslim India. I see from the correspondence and talks between you and me that you are still holding fast to this fateful resolution.

"From the very first day of our talks, you made it clear to me, and you have repeatedly said in the course of our correspondence and talks that you have approached me in your individual capacity, and you assured me that you were a seeker of light and knowledge and that you seriously and earnestly wanted to understand the Lahore Resolution and were open to conviction and conversion. Therefore, in deference to your wishes I made every effort all these days and in the course of our prolonged talks and correspondence to convert you, but unfortunately it seems I have failed. And now you have made new suggestions and proposals by your letter under reply.

"1. You say, 'I have, therefore, suggested a way out. Let it be a partition as between two brothers, if a division there must be'. I really do not know what this means, and I would like you to elaborate this proposal and give me some rough outlines of this new idea of yours, as to how and when the division is to take place, and in what way it is different from the division envisaged by the Lahore Resolution.

"2. You say, 'Let us call in a third party or parties to guide or even arbitrate between us'. May I point out that you have repeatedly made clear to me that you are having these talks as an individual seeker? How can any question of a third party or parties to guide or arbitrate between us arise?"

Gandhiji sent his Id greetings to Jinnah on 23 September: "I was wondering what I shall send you today. It should be fair on my part to let you and your sister share equally the crisp chapattis. They make for me. Here is your share. Please regard it as a token of my love and do please help yourself to it."

24.9.1944

In his letter of September 24, Gandhiji wrote to Jinnah:

"With your assistance I am exploring the possibilities of reaching an agreement, so that the claim embodied in the Muslim League Resolution of Lahore may be reasonably satisfied. You must, therefore, have no apprehensions that the August Resolution will stand in the way of our reaching an agreement. That Resolution dealt with the question of India as against Britain, and it cannot stand in the way of our settlement.

"I proceed on the assumptions that India is not to be regarded as two or more nations, but as one family consisting of many members of whom the Muslims living in the North-West zones, i.e., Baluchistan, Sind, North-West Frontier Province and that part of the Punjab where they are in absolute majority over all the other elements and in parts of Bengal and Assam where they are in absolute majority, desire to live in separation from the rest of India.

"Differing from you on the general basis, I can yet recommend to the Congress and the country the acceptance of the claim for separation contained in the Muslim League Resolution of Lahore, 1940, on my basis and on the following terms:

"The area should be demarcated by a commission, approved by the Congress and the League. The wishes of the inhabitants of the area demarcated should be ascertained through the votes of the adult population of the areas or through some equivalent method.

"If the vote is in favour of separation, it shall be agreed that these areas shall form a separate State as soon as possible after India is free from foreign domination and can, therefore, be constituted into two sovereign independent States.

"There shall be a treaty of separation, which should also provide for the efficient and satisfactory administration of Foreign Affairs, Defence, Internal Communications, Customs, Commerce and the like, which must necessarily continue to be matters of common interest between the contracting parties.

"The treaty shall also contain terms for safeguarding the rights of minorities in the two States.

"Immediately on the acceptance of this agreement by the Congress and the League, the two shall decide upon a common course of action for the attainment of the independence of India.

"The League will, however, be free to remain out of any direct action, to which the Congress may resort and in which the League may not be willing to participate.

"If you do not agree to these terms, could you let me know in precise terms what you would have me to accept in terms of the Lahore Resolution and bind myself to recommend to the Congress? If you could kindly do this, I shall be able to see, apart from the difference in approach, what definite terms I can agree to. In your letter of 23 September, you refer to 'the basis and fundamental principles embodied in the Lahore Resolution' and ask me to accept them. Surely, this is unnecessary, when as I feel, I have accepted the concrete consequence that should follow from such acceptance.

Gandhi and Jinnah also had talks on September 24 as given below:

Jinnah: If you want defence and so many things in common, that means that you visualise a centre?

Gandhiji: No, but I must say, in practice, there will have to be a body selected by both parties to regulate these things.

Then he came to the August 1942 Resolution.

He said that it was inimical to the Muslims.

"But do not you see that it is absolutely a baseless charge? With all the legal acumen that is attributed to you, why cannot you see that it deals with only India and the British rule? It has nothing to do with the Muslims. You can refer the matter to a lawyer of eminence impersonally and take his opinion whether there is anything in it which could be considered inimical to the Muslim League or the Muslims."

He said that he need not to do so. "Why should I want another's opinion when I know it for myself? I broached the subject that I had fixed up to be at Sevagram on the 2 October. I would like to leave on 30 and would be back in four or five days."

He said: "Why must you take so long? We had better close up now. I will have everything ready by Tuesday. You will examine the copies and I will do so."

He had the introduction also ready and read it out.

I said I had nothing to say against it, but if I had a copy I could examine it.

He said I could do so on Tuesday.

I said allright. He would not have a third party, nor would he produce his own scheme. He condemned the August Resolution. He suggested in so many words that amends should be made, i.e., it should be retracted.

Gandhiji sent the following letter to Rajagopalachari on September 25.

"If you are satisfied that my letter of yesterday is the last word you should do the following:

"1. You should ask Jinnah to see you. He told me he has nothing against you, etc. If Bhulabhai has thoroughly understood the position he too may see Jinnah. You may both offer to see him together.

"2. I attach great importance to the legal opinion on Jinnah's interpretation of the August Resolution.

"3. It may be wise to call in Shivarao, if you have not done so already."

25.9.1944

Jinnah sent a letter to Gandhiji on September 25, in which he said:

"I am in receipt of your of September 24 and I thank you for it.

"You have already rejected the basic and fundamental principles of the Lahore Resolution.

"1. You do not accept that the Musalmans of India are a nation.

"2. You do not accept that the Musalmans have an inherent right of self-determination.

"3. You do not accept that they alone are entitled to exercise this right of theirs for self-determination.

"4. you do not accept that Pakistan is composed of two zones, north-west and north-east, comprising six provinces, namely, Sind, Baluchistan, North-West Frontier Provinces, Punjab, Bengal and Assam, subject to territorial adjustments that may be agreed upon, as indicated in the Lahore Resolution. The matter of demarcating and defining the territories can be taken up after the fundamentals above mentioned are accepted, and for that purpose, machinery may be set up by agreement.

"You do not accept the provisions embodied in the Lahore Resolution for safeguarding the minorities. I asked you to give me rough outlines of this new idea of yours as to how and when the division is to take place and in what way it is different from the division envisaged in the Lahore Resolution, and now you have been good enough to give me your amplification, in your letter of September 24 under reply.

"The terms clearly indicate that your basis is in vital conflict with and is opposed to the fundamental basis and principles of the Lahore Resolution. Now let me take your main terms:

"a) I proceed on the assumption that India is not to be regarded as two or more nations, but as one family consisting of many members, of whom the Muslims living in the north-west zones, i.e. Baluchistan, Sind, North-West Frontier Province and later part of the Punjab where they are in absolute majority over all the other elements and in parts of Bengal and Assam where they are in absolute majority, desire to live in separation from the rest of India. If these terms were accepted and given effect to, the present boundaries of these Provinces would be maimed and mutilated beyond redemption and leave us only with the husk, and it is opposed to the Lahore Resolution.

"b) That even in these mutilated areas so defined, the right of self-determination will not be exercised by the Muslims but by inhabitants of these areas so demarcated. This again is opposed to the fundamentals of the Lahore Resolution.

"c) That if the vote is in favor of separation, they shall be followed to 'form a separate State as soon as possible after India is free from foreign domination.' We propose that we should come to a complete settlement of our own immediately and by our united front and efforts do everything in our power to secure freedom and independence of the peoples of India on the basis of Pakistan and Hindustan.

"d) Next you say, 'There shall be a treaty of separation which should also provide for the efficient and satisfactory administration of Foreign Affairs, Defence, Internal Communications, Customs, Commerce, and the like, which must necessarily continue to be matters of common interest between the contracting parties.' If these vital matters are to be administered by some central authority, you do not indicate what sort of authority or machinery will be set up to administer these matters, and how and to whom again that authority will be responsible. All these matters, which are the life-blood of any State, cannot be delegated to any central authority or government. The matter of the security of the two States and the natural and mutual obligations that may arise out of physical contiguity will be for the constitution-making body of Pakistan and that of Hindustan, or any other party concerned, to deal with on the footing of their being two independent States. As regards the safeguarding of the rights of minorities, I have already explained that this question of safeguarding the minorities is fully stated in the Lahore Resolution.

"You will, therefore, see that the entire basis of your new proposal is fundamentally opposed to the Lahore Resolution, and as I have already pointed out to you both in the correspondence and in our discussions, it is very difficult for me to entertain counter-proposals and negotiate, unless they come from you in your representative capacity. That was the same difficulty with regard to the Gandhi-Rajaji Formula, and I made it clear to you, at the very outset, but the Formula was discussed as you asserted it had met the Lahore resolution in substance. But while you were furnishing me with clarification of this Formula, you shunted it and we confined ourselves to the Lahore Resolution, and hence the question of your representative capacity did not arise regarding this Formula. But now you have, in your letter of September 24, made a new proposal of your own on your own basis, and the same difficulties present themselves to me as before, and it is difficult to deal with it any further unless it comes from you in your representative capacity.

"I cannot agree with you when you finally wind up by saying: 'In your letter of 23 September, you refer to the basic and fundamental principles embodied in the Lahore Resolution and ask me to accept them. Surely, this is unnecessary when as I feel I have accepted the concrete consequence that should follow from such acceptance.' This is obviously far from correct. Why not then accept the fundamentals of the Lahore Resolution and proceed to settle the details?"

25.9.1944

Gandhiji also sent the draft of his following letter, to Rajaji, which was sent to Jinnah on September 25.

"Yesterday's talk leads me to inflict this letter on you, which I trust you will not mind.

"Our conversations have come about as a result of your correspondence with Rajaji in July last over his Formula and your consultations with the League Working

Committee thereon, and my own letter to you suggesting a meeting between you and me. My proposal of yesterday is an earnest effort to meet the essential requirements of the Lahore Resolution. I would like you, therefore, to think fifty times before throwing away an offer which had been made entirely in the spirit of service in the cause of communal harmony. Do not take, I pray, the responsibility of rejecting the offer. Throw it on your Council. Give me an opportunity of addressing them. If they feel like rejecting it, I would like you to advice the Council to put it before the open session of the League. If you will accept my advice and permit me, I would attend the open session and address it.

"You are too technical when you dismiss my proposal for arbitration or outside guidance over points of difference. If I have approached you as an individual, and not in any representative capacity, it is because we believe that if I reach an agreement with you, it will be of material use in the process of securing a Congress-League settlement and acceptance of it by the country. It is irrelevant or inadmissible to supplement our efforts to convince each other without help, guidance, advice or even arbitration?"

26.9.1944

Jinnah in his letter of September 26 to Gandhiji said:

I am in receipt of your letter of September 25. It is entirely incorrect and has no foundation in fact, for you to say that our conversations have come about as a result of my correspondence with Rajaji in July last over his Formula. It is equally baseless to say 'and your consultations with the League Working Committee thereon.' It was entirely in response to your letter of July 17, 1944, which I received while I was at Srinagar, with a fervent request on your part to meet you, and you ended that letter by saying, 'Do not dismiss me.' In my reply, again from Srinagar, dated July 24, 1944, I intimated to you that I would be glad to receive you at my house in Bombay on my return, which would probably about the middle of August. This was long before the meeting of the Working Committee or that of the Council of the All-India Muslim League, and long before I reached Lahore, and when you arrived here and told me that you were approaching me in your individual capacity, I at once made it clear to you and informed you, both in our talks and letter, that the position you have taken up had no precedent for it, and further that it was not possible to negotiate and reach an agreement unless both the parties were fully represented. For, it is one-sided business, as it will not be binding upon any organisation in any sense whatever, but you would as an individual only recommend it, if any agreement is reached, to the Congress and the country, whereas it would be binding upon me as the President of the Muslim League. I cannot accept this position. I hope you do see the unfairness and the great disadvantage to me, and it is so simple and elementary for anyone to understand.

"As regards your proposal of yesterday, which you have simplified in your letter of September 24, I have already sent you my reply.

"With regard to your suggestion to be allowed to address the meeting of the Council, and if they feel like rejecting your 'offer' the matter should be put up before the open session, let me inform you that only a member or delegate is entitled to participate in the deliberations of the meetings of the Council or the open session respectively. Besides, it is a most extraordinary and unprecedented suggestion to make. However, I thank you for your advice.

"As regards your proposal for arbitration and outside guidance, I have already replied to you, and it is not merely technical but a matter of substance. I fully reciprocate your desire for securing a Congress-League settlement.

"However, I regret I have failed to convince you, as I was hopeful of doing."

26 September 1944

Gandhiji wrote a letter to Jinnah on September 26 in which he said: "In view of my letter to you of yesterday, left to myself, I would have refrained from dealing with your letter before our meeting today. But I have deferred to Rajaji's advice to finish the chain of correspondence.

"I confess I am unable to understand your persistent refusal to appreciate the fact that the Formula presented to you by me in my letter of the 24 as well as the Formula presented to you by Rajaji give virtually what is embodied in the Lahore Resolution, providing at the same time what is absolutely necessary to make the arrangement acceptable to the country. You keep on saying that I should accept certain theses, while I have been contending that the best way for us, who differ in our approach to the problem, is to give body to the demand as it stands in the Resolution and work it out to our mutual satisfaction. It is on this plan that I understand Rajaj's Formula is to be conceived, and it is on the same plan that I have tried to work it out in the course of and as a result of our talks. I contend that either gives you the substance of the Lahore Resolution. Unfortunately, you reject both. And I cannot accept the Lahore Resolution as you want me to, especially when you seek to introduce into its interpretation theories and claims which I cannot accept and which I cannot ever hope to induce India to accept.

"Your constant references to my not being clothed with representative authority are really irrelevant. I have approached you so that, if you and I can agree upon a common course of action, I may use what influence I may possess for its acceptance by the Congress and the country. If you break, it cannot be because I have no representative capacity, or because I have been unwilling to give you satisfaction in regard to the claim embodied in the Lahore Resolution."

26.9.1944

Jinnah sent his following letter to Gandhiji on September 26:

I have received your letter of September 26 and I note that you have written it with Rajaji's advice. Of course, it is for you to follow such advice as you may choose to do, but I am only concerned for the moment with you. I note that at the last moment you have resurrected the Gandhi-Rajaji Formula, although it was shunted all this time and you proceed to say that this Formula gives me virtually what is embodied in the Lahore Resolution. You further say that on the same plan you have tried to formulate your latest proposals, as mentioned in your letter of September 24 and you maintain that either gives me the substance of the Lahore Resolution. In your previous letter you asserted that your Formula gives me the 'essence' of the Lahore Resolution. I see a very close family resemblance between the two, and the substance of one or the other is practically the same, only it is put in different language, and I have already expressed my opinion, that in my judgment they neither meet the substance nor the essence of the Lahore Resolution. On the contrary, both are calculated to completely torpedo the Pakistan demand of Muslim India.

I have never asked you to accept certain theses nor have I introduced any theories in the Lahore Resolution. Theses and theories are matters for scholars to indulge in.

"I am very sorry I have to repeat, but I am compelled to do so, that I cannot agree with you that my references to your not being clothed with representative authority are really irrelevant. On the contrary, they have an important bearing, as I have already explained to you more than once. You again repeat that if you and I can agree upon a common course of action, you may use what influence you may possess for its acceptance by the Congress and the country. I have already stated from the very beginning that that is not enough, for the reasons I have already given. Your representative capacity comes into play when you are making counter-proposals, and I cannot understand how you can say that it is irrelevant. No responsible organisation can entertain any proposal from any individual, howsoever great he may be, unless it is backed up with the authority of a recognised organisation, and comes from its fully accredited representative. However, I need not labor this point any more, as I have already explained it in our previous correspondence.

"If a break comes, it will be because you have not satisfied me in regard to the essence of the claim embodied in the Lahore Resolution. It is not a question of your being unwilling, but in fact, it is so. If a break comes it will be most unfortunate, if one does not agree with you or differs from you, you are always right and the other party is always wrong, and the next thing is that many are waiting prepared, in your circle, to pillory me when the word goes, but I must face all threats and consequences, and I can only act according to my judgment and conscience."

27.9.1944

Jinnah's Statement

Jinnah issued the following statement to the press on September 27:

"Mr. Gandhi, from the very commencement of our talks, made it clear that he had approached me in his individual capacity and that he represented no one but himself. However, he assured me that he was open to conviction and conversion to the Muslim League Lahore Resolution of March 1940.

"Without prejudice to my objection that in order to reach any settlement, negotiations can only be carried on properly when the other side is also fully represented and vested with authority, in deference to Mr. Gandhi's wishes I agreed to the task of persuading and converting him to the fundamentals of the Lahore Resolution.

"I have placed before him everything and every aspect of the Muslim point of view in the course of our prolonged talks and correspondence, and we discussed all the pros and cons generally, and I regret to say that I have failed in my task of converting Mr. Gandhi.

"We have, therefore, decided to release to the press the correspondence that has passed between us.

"Nevertheless, we hope that the public will not feel embittered, and we trust that this is not the final end of our effort."

27.9.1944

In his prayer meeting on September 27, referring to the leakage of the correspondence between him and Qaid-e-Azam and its unauthorised publication in a certain section of the press, Gandhiji observed that he had warned the press before against indulging in conjectures, because he felt that would damage the cause. But what had appeared in the press now was more than a mere conjecture. It seemed that they had somewhat managed to get actual copies of the correspondence. Perhaps it was clever on their part, but that did them little credit. Journalism, like every institution, had its own code of ethics and he was not there to pass judgment. All he could say was that he himself had, perhaps, followed a different code of ethics even in the field of journalism.

He assured them that the leakage had not occurred from his office, and he had strong reasons for his belief. He had the other day drawn the Qaid-e-Azam's attention to the leakage, but the Qaid-e-Azam was indifferent. Public men had to cultivate that indifference, or else life would become impossible. But it was for the public not to take relish in such happenings. If the public strongly disapproved all such practices, the press would not repeat them. It was intolerable that anyone should try to pry into and give publicity to private correspondence without authority.

He told them that when the talks were over, he would let them know the result. That stage had been reached yesterday, but as the copies of the correspondence were not ready, its actual release had to be postponed till today. Authorised copies of the correspondence had now been sent to the press with a prefatory statement by the Qaid-e-Azam.

Hitherto he had told them that he was not without hope with regard to the outcome of the talks. He had to confess that the result that he was hoping for had not materialised. But he had no sense of disappointment or despondency. He was convinced that even out of that break down good would result.

Although Qaid-e-Azam and he had known each other fairly well in public life before, they had not come into such personal contact. Their conversations were carried out with friendliness and cordiality. He wanted all the communities to cultivate the same spirit of friendliness and cordiality in their relations with one another. They should try to convert one another through it.

They might ask, "Why was it then that he and Qaid-e-Azam had failed to convert each other?" His reply was that he had tried his level best to go as far as he could to meet the Qaid-e-Azam's viewpoint. He had taken incalculable pains to understand him and to make himself understood. But he had failed.

He had placed before the Qaid-e-Azam Rajaji's Formula, but that did not commend itself to him. He had thereupon put forth another proposal of his own in its place, but even that had failed to secure Jinnah Saheb's approval. In the same way, Jinnah Saheb's proposal had failed to commend itself to him. If either of them had been weak, they would have possibly come to some sort of agreement, but as responsible men they could not afford to be weak. A helmsman had to be firm and unwavering, or else the ship would founder upon the rocks. Each one of them had tried to convince the other. It was possible that both of them might be in the wrong. But so long as each felt himself to be in the right, he could not let go his hold.

The news of breakdown, he knew, would cause grief to the friends of India and might give cause for jubilation to their enemies.

Although they had been unable to appreciate each other's viewpoint, the public could help them to do so. They should not lose heart, If there was anyone who had reason to feel disappointed it was he. He had knocked at the Qaid-e-Azam's door. But he had already observed there was no despondency in him, It was not for a votary of truth and non-violence to feel despondent if his effort at times failed to yield the result aimed at. Failure should only serve as a spur to further effort. God alone knew what was best for them. It was not for them to question God's ways. Therefore, instead of feeling despondent, they should regard the breakdown as a challenge to their faith and as an incentive for greater effort for establishing true unity among the various communities.

28-9-1944

A Press Conference of about 40 Indian and Foreign journalists was held at Birla House. Sarojini Naidu, Rajagopalachari, Bhulabhai Desai, Nagindas Master, M.Y. Nurie, Dr. M.D.D. Gilder, and S. K. Patil were among others present. Gandhiji read out his following statement:

"It is a matter of deep regret that we two could not reach an agreement. But there is no cause for disappointment. The break-down is only so-called. It is an adjournment *sine die.* Each one of us must now talk to public and put our viewpoints before them. If we do so dispassionately and if the public co-operate, we may reach a solution of the seemingly insoluble at an early date. My experience of the previous three weeks confirms me in the view that a presence of a third power hinders the solution. A mind enslaved cannot act as if it was free. I need not impute base motives to the rulers to prove what seems to me to be an axiomatic truth. Nevertheless, I am going to continue to work for the solution as I have been during these three weeks. The questions for consideration are simple. Has the Rajaji Formula or mine made a reasonable approach to the Lahore Resolution? If they or either of them is such an approach, all parties, and especially the members of the

Muslim League, should ask the Quid-e-Azam to revise his opinion. If Rajaji and I have stultified the Lahore Resolution we should be educated. The chief thing is for the press and the public to avoid partisanship and bitterness."

To a question on his future plans, whether he proposed to concentrate on a Hindu-Muslim settlement or take up political work, seeking imprisonment if necessary, Mahatma Gandhi replied: "I shall act as my inner voice tells me."

Asked how far the offer he had made conceded the demand made in the Lahore Resolution of the League, Mahatma emphasized that the Rajaji Formula or the formula he presented consisted the substance of the League demand. He said:

"In my opinion, either formula gives as much as can reasonably be expected with due regard to the interests of the whole of India."

In answer to a question whether his offer was to be treated now as withdrawn, he said that so far as he was concerned the offer he had made stood. It was not made in any bargaining spirit. He said:

"I think it is a just solution of the problem and it is in the spirit of the policy which the Congress has consistently adopted in connection with the communal question, namely, self-determination."

A number of questions were put on the representative character of the two leaders who conducted the negotiations and why Mahatma Gandhi prolonged the talks when he was apprised of Mr. Jinnah's views on the first day of the talks.

Mahatma Gandhi answered: "I am a man reputed to have inexhaustible patience and I had no reason to despair of either being converted by the Qaid-e-Azam or in my turn converting him. Therefore, so long as there was the slightest possibility, I clung to the hope that we shall pull through a solution. Haste in such cases is a most dangerous thing. You should, therefore, conclude that yesterday was really a moment when the public should have been taken into confidence. As for myself, I am entirely satisfied that we have not wasted these three weeks. I have no doubt whatsoever that we know now each other better than ever before.

"When you agreed to meet Jinnah, did you meet him on the basis that he was the sole representative of the Muslims?

"I have never admitted that claim, but I have said throughout that the Muslim League is by far the most representative Muslim organisation. It would have been folly on my part not to recognise this, but I have always been aware that there is outside the League a large body of Muslims which does not see eye to eye with the League and which does not believe in the two nations theory."

Mahatma Gandhi asserted that the fight for freedom had not been suspended when he approached the Qaid-e-Azam. He said: "My approach to the Qaid-e-Azam was itself a part of the fight for freedom."

Asked if there was any possibility of the two leaders meeting again in the near future, Mahatma Gandhi said: "I hope so. It is for the press and the public to make it possible and hasten the date. I assure you that we have not parted as enemies, but as friends."

"If the Rjaji Formula or his own formula had conceded the substance of the Lahore Resolution, then why not agree to the Resolution itself?

"Although the resolution does not say so, if you study the correspondence, it shows that it is based on the two nations theory and it has known as the Pakistan Resolution. Further, I had to examine the Resolution in view of the interpretation put upon it by the Qaid-e-Azam in his numerous speeches and statements in elucidation of the Resolution. It is undisputable that the Resolution, while it does not enunciate that theory, is based upon that theory. The Qaid-e-Azam has insisted upon that. Therefore, I urge that apart from the two nations theory, if I could accept the principle of the division of India in accordance with the demand of the League, he should accept it. But it was unfortunate it was just there we split."

Mahatma Gandhi was asked what he thought of the idea of formation of provinces on linguistic, cultural and communal basis. He replied that since 1920 he was for provinces on a linguistic basis. As for redistribution on a cultural basis, he did not really know what it meant and he was unable to understand how provinces could be reconstituted on communal lines unless there was a suggestion that there should be inter-migration of the various communities to concentrate into particular areas. It seemed to him to be fantastic and impossible.

He said: We are not inhabiting a country full of deserts and wastelands. We are a densely populated country and I do not see the slightest chance for such redistribution. In that respect the Lahore Resolution is quite sound—where there is an obvious Muslim majority they should be allowed to constitute a separate State by themselves and that has been fully conceded in the Rajaji Formula or my formula. There is nothing much distinction between them. That right is conceded without the slightest reservation. But if it means utterly independent sovereignty so that there is to be nothing in common between the two, I hold it is an impossible proposition. That means war to the knife. It is not a proposition that resolves itself into a voluntary or friendly solution.

"Therefore, the Rajaji Formula or my formula has presented certain things to be in common between sovereign States. Therefore, there is no question of one party overbearing the other or the center having an overbearing Hindu majority. I think our formula should be critically and sympathetically examined and it would be found that the formula concedes everything that could reasonably be conceded if we consider ourselves to be one family. Children of the same family, dissatisfied with one another by reason of change of religion, if they should separate, then the separation should be within ourselves and not separation in the face of the whole world. When two brothers separate, they do not become enemies of one another in the eyes of the world. The world will still recognise them as brothers."

Some journalists said that some of the nationalist Muslims felt that the Congress through Mahatma Gandhi meeting Mr. Jinnah had put them in a false position and that they might have to change their attitude towards Indian nationalism.

Mahatma Gandhi replied that it was an extraordinary suggestion. Nationalist Muslims were nationalists simply because they could not be otherwise. He said: "I am a nationalist, not in order to please anybody, but because I cannot be otherwise. And if I approached the Qaid-e-Azam, I approach him in the common interests of myself and nationalist Muslims and other nationalists. Nationalist Muslims, so far as I know, were delighted when I approached the Qaid-e-Azam and were looking forward to a proper solution in the confidence that I would not sell the interests represented by them.

"Undoubtedly, a nationalist Muslim represents the nation, but he represents the Muslims also, who are a part of the nation. He would be guilty of disloyalty, if he sacrifices the Muslim interest. But my nationalism has taught me that I would be guilty of disloyalty if I sacrifice the interests of a single Indian."

Asked if there was any difference between his present attitude towards the Muslim League demand and the stand he took in 1942, Mahatma Gandhi said: There is very great difference. In 1942, Rajaji had not 'burst' on the scene as he did at the Agha Khan Palace with a concrete proposition. It reflects very great credit on his persistence. He never takes up a standpoint without the fullest consideration and having taken it up, he follows it to the bitterest end. He had abundant faith in my loyalty and he never gave me up as I have never given him up. When he found me in the Agha Khan palace and presented the Formula, I did not take even five minutes and I said 'yes' because I saw it in a concrete shape.

"My mind is narrow. I have not read much literature. I have not seen much of the world. I have concentrated upon certain things in life and beyond that I have no other interest. Therefore, I could not realise the meaning of Rajaji's stand and I disliked it. But when he came with a concrete formula—I myself am a concrete being of flesh and blood—and when he had put something in concrete shape, I felt I could hug it and touch it. Therefore, you see the vast difference between 1942 and today. However, thereby I have not departed from the Congress standpoint in general terms. Congress has accepted self-determination and therefore the Formula had become common ground."

Interview to *News Chronicle*

In his interview to Stuart Gilder of *News Chronicle*, London, on September 29, Gandhiji told him as to why his talks with Jinnah failed to produce a solution of the Hindu-Muslim differences.

"I could not accept the two nations basis. This was Mr. Jinnah's demand. He wants immediate recognition of the North-West Frontier Province, Sind, whole of the Punjab, Bengal and Assam as sovereign and completely independent Pakistan."

He wants Mr. Jinnah to agree to this amputation from the rest of India without consulting the wishes of the inhabitants by plebiscite. He has rejected the Rajaji Formula. "I asked Mr. Jinnah what he was prepared to recognise as Pakistan and on what basis there could be any hope of agreement in future. He was frank and precise."

Gandhi said: "I want to make it clear that I believe Mr. Jinnah is sincere, but I think he is suffering from hallucination when he imagines that an unnatural division of India could bring either happiness or prosperity to the people concerned. It was my suggestion that provided there was the safeguard of plebiscite there could be sovereignty for the predominantly Muslim areas, but it should be accompanied by bonds of alliance between Hindustan and Pakistan. There should be common policy and working arrangement on foreign affairs, defence, communications and similar matters. This is manifestly vital to the welfare of both parts of India."

This arrangement, Mr. Gandhi said, could not interfere with the internal life of Muslims who would not be subject to anyway to Hindu domination. Such a division would not create an artificial split between people who, whatever their religious faiths are, descended from a common stock and are all Indians.

"Unfortunately Mr. Jinnah would have none of it and asked me to agree to the principle of two nations entirely separate."

I asked Mr. Gandhi if he had adopted the attitude because he thought he could not 'sell' such a division to the country or because he thought it wrong in principle. He replied: "Because, it is fundamentally wrong in principle. If I had thought Mr. Jinnah's view was right, even the whole world were against me, I would have accepted it personally and given him my unquestioned allegiance."

"If Mr. Jinnah agreed to your view of division, but insisted there should be no plebiscite or a plebiscite in which only Muslims would vote, would you settle on this basis?"

N"ever. How could I agree in personal or any other capacity to decide the future of millions of people without their having anything to say about their destiny?"

"What was your impression of Mr. Jinnah's attitude on the question of an interim government which you outlined to me in July?"

"Mr. Jinnah has said that he is deeply interested in independence, but it did not seem to me that he set as great store by it as immediate recognition of the Pakistan he wants. Whereas, you see, my view has been all along that we cannot be free among ourselves until we are free from imperial domination. We have parted as friends. These days have not been wasted. I am convinced that Mr. Jinnah is a good man. I hope we shall meet again. I am a man of prayer and I shall pray for understanding. In the meantime, it is the duty of the people to digest the situation and bring the pressure of their opinion upon us."

M.R. Jayakar wrote a letter to Gandhi on September 30, in which he said: "So your talks have failed. I am not surprised. There could be no meeting-ground between you two. Your efforts have now ended and I suppose I am at liberty now to express my sentiments on the nature and result of your effort if I choose to do so. It is frankly my opinion that the Muslim League leader has gained more from you than he has lost to you. Your formula is in Mr. Jinnah's hands and he will use this formula as a bargaining counter with the British Government and also as the starting point in future negotiations with Indian leaders. If at such negotiations Mr. Jinnah revives the Formula, you will be powerless to resist it. Therein lies the danger in my opinion. To me, Jinnah would prefer a settlement with the British, rather than with his own countrymen."

Gandhiji replied to Jayakar on September 30: "I did what I thought the best for the country. Of course, you should now express yourself freely on the question. That way only we shall arrive at the truth.

"I am preparing for my departure and writing this against time. Hence this brief note."

And Gandhi left for Wardha on September 30, 1944.

5

Reactions to the Failure of the Gandhi-Jinnah Talks

The breakdown of the Gandhi-Jinnah talks provoked world-wide reactions. Pethic Lawrence, the British Labour M.P., said: "I feel sure that I am not poisoning the sentiments of many people in this country (England) in expressing the regret at the news that the two distinguished statesmen of India have not found it possible so far to reach an agreement."

Pearls S.Buck, a noted American novelist, remarked in New York: "I consider it as a tragedy for India and England but for all the United Nations."

J.J. Singh, President of the India League in America and in London, expressed disappointment at the failure of the talks. N.R. Sarkar, an ex-member of the Viceroy's Executive Council, significantly said that "the tragedy of the situation is that there is no means now open to us for retrieving the position since the Congress cannot formally meet to consider the situation resulting from the failure of the talks." The Liberal leaders like Setalwad and Chandavarkar commented that they did not regret the breakdown of the negotiation because it was based on the vicious principle of the partition of Hindustan and Pakistan.

N.B. Khare of the Hindu Mahasabha, Allama Mashriqi, the Khaksar leader, and M.N. Roy, the Radical Democratic Party leader, hoped that the failure of the talks would lead to a fresh examination of the problem that would enable the Indian leaders to find a practical solution to the problem of achieving the freedom of India and preserving its unity. Various news papers like the *Statesman* wrote that the talks broke down not because of any external interference but because there was no initial agreement between the two. The *Dawn*, which represented the Muslim League's point of view, significantly remarked that the failure of the talks clearly showed that Rajagopalachari had not really succeeded in winning over Gandhiji to accepting Pakistan. The *Hindustan Standard* also commented that Mahatma Gandhi, in these talks, clearly showed that he did not accept the two-nation theory and that the Rajaji Formula should once and for all be given up.

Dr. Shyama Prasad Mookerjee

The Hindu Mahasabha leader, Dr. Shyama Prasad Mookerjee, felt that in these talks Jinnah came close to making Gandhi agree to the partition of India at least in principle. The talks went on for several days, which clearly showed that Gandhi and Jinnah could not agree. The failure of the unity talks was unfortunate because the British Government insisted on an agreement between all sections of Indians before independence could be granted.

B.R. Nanda

Commenting on the failure of the talks B.R.Nanda said: "While these conversations were no more than a kind of a re-education for Gandhi, they brought an accession of political strength to Jinnah. That Gandhiji had knocked at his door raised Jinnah's prestige. The fact that the Mahatma had relented so far as to discuss the machinery for the exercise of the right of self-determination for the Muslims, was a feather in Jinnah's cap."

Maulana Abul Kalam Azad

"Gandhij's approach to Jinnah was a great political blunder. It gave a new and added importance to Jinnah, which he latter exploited fully. Jinnah had lost much of his political importance after he left the Congress in the twenties. It was largely due to Gandhiji's acts of commission and omission that Jinnah regained his importance in Indian political life. In fact, it is doubtful if Jinnah could have ever achieved a supremacy, but for Gandhiji's attitude. Large sections of Indian Muslims were doubtful about Mr. Jinnah and his policy, but when they found that Gandhiji was continuously running after him and entreating him, many of them developed a new respect for Jinnah. They also thought that Jinnah was perhaps the best man for getting advantageous terms in the communal settlement." Azad further writes: "It was Gandhiji who first gave currency to the title Qaid-e-Azam or great leader as applied to Mr. Jinnah. Gandhiji had in his camp a foolish but well-intentioned girl called Amtus Salam. She had seen in some Urdu papers a reference to Jinnah as Qaid-e-Azam. When Gandhiji was writing to Jinnah asking for interview, she told him that the Urdu papers called Jinnah Qaid-e-Azam and he should use the same form of address. Without pausing to consider the implications of his action, Gandhiji addressed Jinnah as Qaid-e-Azam. This letter was soon after published in the press. When Indian Muslims saw that Gandhiji also addressed Jinnah as Qaid-e-Azam, they felt that he must really be so. When in July 1944, I read the report that Gandhiji was corresponding with Jinnah and going to Bombay to meet him, I told my collegues that Gandhiji was making a great mistake. His action would not help to solve but on the contrary would aggravate the Indian political situation. Later events proved that my apprehensions were correct. Jinnah exploited the situation fully and built up his own position, but he did not say or do anything, which could in any way help the cause of Indian freedom." (*India Wins Freedom:* Maulana Abul Kalam Azad, pp.96-97)

Sir Tej Bahadur Sapru

Tej Bahadur Sapru was greatly disappointed and anguished on the failure of the Gandhi-Jinnah talks. He wrote to Pyarelal: "Personally, I think Gandhiji handled the problem very efficiently. It is absurd for Mr. Jinnah to insist on the two nation theory. (*Tej Bahadur Sapru,* S. K. Bose, pp.151)

Justice M.C. Chagla

M.C. Chagla, a patriotic Muslim, who rose to the position of the Chief Justice of Bombay High Court and later Education Minister in the Central Cabinet and Ambassador of India to the United States observed: "Jinnah cared entirely for himself and for none else." Chagla spoke with authority because he had worked in Jinnah's Chambers in Bombay for six years and had long held him as his *Beau Ideal.* Chagla asked Jinnah what would happen to Indian Muslims after the country's division. Jinnah looked at him for a while and said: "They will look after themselves. I am not interested in their fate." (*Roses in December, M.C. Chagla,* pp. 80)

Dr. K.M. Munshi

"Gandhiji, I felt, was committing a mistake in seeking an interview with Jinnah, who was inflexible in his objective.

"Rajaji's Formula envisaged Pakistan with a transfer of population. If Gandhiji had been his normal self physically, or if Jawaharlal Nehru and Sardar Patel had been with him, I am sure he would not have anything to do with Rajaji's Formula. He was feeling lonely, and the deep void created in his life by the death of Kasturba and Mahadev Desai had its effect on him.

"Had Rajaji known Jinnah better, he would have seen that the latter's object in getting an interview with Gandhiji was only to secure a spectacular triumph which would add to his prestige as the dominating factor in Indian politics.

"As I look back, I see that if settlement had taken place in 1944, Jinnah would have got away with the whole of the Punjab, Bengal and Assam, with a corridor from East to West Pakistan. (K.M. Munshi, *Pilgrimage to Freedom,* pp.91-92)

Munshiji again in his 'Pilgrimage to Freedom' writes: "The A.I.C.C. in its meeting of April 29, 1942, not only rejected Rajaji's proposals, but adopted a counter resolution, moved by Jagatnarain Lal, insisting on the preservation of the unity of India. The resolution was not on the Agenda but was sponsored by 60 members and was passed by 92 votes against 17.

"The attempt of Rajaji, knowing as he did the mood and temper of his colleagues in the Congress High Command, to convert them on a crucial issue by passing such a resolution in Madras, had far reaching repercussions. It strengthened Jinnah's position and broke the morale of the nationalists on this issue." (K. M. Munshi, *Pilgrimage to Freedom,* pp. 80-81)

Dr. B.R. Ambedkar

Dr, Ambedkar analysed the failure of Gandhi-Jinnah talks as follows: "The failure of Gandhi-Jinnah talks produced different reactions in the minds of different people. Some were glad, others were sorry. But as both had been, just previous to the talks, worsted by their opponents in their struggle for supremacy, Gandhi by the British and Jinnah by the Unionist Party in the Punjab, and had lost a good deal of their credit the majority of people expected that they would put forth some constructive effort to bring about a solution.

The failure may have been due to the defects of personalities. But it must however be said that failure was inevitable having regard to certain fundamental faults in the C.R. Formula. In the first place, it tied up the communal question with the political question in an indissoluble knot. No political settlement, no communal settlement, is the strategy on which the formula proceeds. The formula did not offer a solution. It invited Mr. Jinnah to enter into a deal. It was a bargain—"If you help us in getting independence, we shall be glad to consider your proposal for Pakistan." I do not know from where Mr. Rajagopalachariar got the idea that this was the best means of getting independence. It is possible that he borrowed it from the old Hindu kings of India who built up alliance for protecting their independence against foreign enemies by giving their daughters to neighboring princes. Mr. Rajagopalachariar forgot that such alliances brought neither a good husband nor a permanent ally.

"To make communal settlement depend upon help rendered in winning freedom is a very unwise way of proceeding in a matter of this kind. It is a way of one party drawing another party into its net by offering communal privileges as a bait. The C.R. Formula made communal settlement an article for sale."

"The second fault in the C.R. Formula relates to the machinery for giving effect to any agreement that may be arrived at. The agency suggested in the C.R. Formula is the Provisional Government. In suggesting this Mr. Rajagopalachariar obviously overlooked two difficulties. The first thing he overlooked is that once the Provisional Government was established, the promises of the contracting parties, to use legal phraseology, did not remain concurrent promises. The case became one of the executed promise against executory promise. By consenting to the establishment of a Provisional Government, the League would have executed its promise to help the Congress to win independence. But the promise of the Congress to bring about Pakistan would remain executory.

Mr. Jinnah who insists, and quite rightly, that the promise should be concurrent could never be expected to agree to place himself in such a position. The second difficulty which Mr. Rajagopachariar has overlooked is what would happen if the Provisional Government failed to give effect to the Congress part of the agreement. Who is to enforce it? The Provisional Government is to be sovereign Government, not subject to superior authority. If it was unwilling to give effect to the agreement, the only sanction open to the Muslims would be rebellion. To make the Provisional Government the agency for forging a new constitution, for bringing about Pakistan, nobody will accept. It is a snare and not a solution. The only way of bringing about the constitutional changes will be through an Act of Parliament embodying provisions agreed upon by the important elements in the national life of British India. There is no other way.

"There is a third fault in the C.R. Formula. It relates to a provision for a treaty between Pakistan and Hindustan to safeguard what are called matters of common interests such as Defence, Foreign Affairs, Customs, etc. Here again Mr. Rajagopalachariar does not seem to be aware of obvious difficulties. How are matters of common interests to be safeguarded? I see only two ways. One is to have Central Government vested with Executive and Legislative authority in respect of these matters. This means Pakistan and Hindustan will not be sovereign States. Will Mr. Jinnah agree to this? Obviously he does not. The other way is to make Pakistan and Hindustan sovereign States and to bind them by a treaty relating to matters of common interests. But what is there to ensure that the terms of the treaty will be observed? As a sovereign State, Pakistan can always repudiate it even if it was a Dominion. Mr. Rajagopalachariar obviously drew his inspiration in drafting this clause from the Anglo-Irish Treaty of 1922. But he forgot the fact that the treaty lasted so long as Ireland was not a Dominion and that as soon as it became a Dominion it repudiated the treaty and the British Parliament stood silent and grinned, for it knew that it could do nothing.

"One does not mind very much that the talks failed. What one feels sorry for is that the talks failed giving us a clear idea of some of the questions about which Mr. Jinnah has been observing discreet silence in his public utterances, though he has been quite outspoken about them in his private talks. These questions are—

"1. Is Pakistan to be conceded because of the Resolution of the Muslim League?

"2. Are the Muslims, as distinguished from the Muslim League, to have no say in the matter?

"3. What will be the boundaries of Pakistan? Whether the boundaries will be the present administrative boundaries of the Punjab and Bengal or whether the boundaries of Pakistan will be ethnological boundaries?

"4. What do the words 'subject to such territorial adjustments as may be necessary' which occur in the Lahore Resolution mean? What were the territorial adjustments the League had in mind?

"5. What does the word 'finally' which, occurs in the last part of the Lahore Resolution mean? Did the League contemplate a transition period in which Pakistan will not be an independent and sovereign State?

"6. If Mr. Jinnah's proposal that the boundaries of Eastern and Western Pakistan are to be the present administrative boundaries, will he allow the Scheduled Castes, or, if I may say so, the non-Muslims in the Punjab and Bengal to determine by a plebiscite whether they wish to be included in Mr. Jinnah's Pakistan and whether Mr. Jinnah would be prepared to abide by the results of the plebiscite of the non-Muslim elements in the Punjab and Bengal?

"7. Does Mr. Jinnah want a corridor running through U.P. and Bihar to connect up Eastern Pakistan to

> Western Pakistan? It would have been a great gain if straight questions had been put to Mr. Jinnah and unequivocal answers obtained. But instead of coming to grips with Mr. Jinnah on these questions, Mr. Gandhi spent his whole time proving that the C.R. Formula is substantially the same as the League's Lahore Resolution—which was ingenious if not nonsensical and thereby lost the best opportunity he had of having these questions clarified.

"After these talks Mr. Gandhi and Mr. Jinnah have retired to their pavilions as players in a cricket match do after their game is over, as though there is nothing further to be done. There is no indication whether they will meet again and if so when. What next? Is not a question which seems to worry them. Yet it is difficult to see how India can make any political advance without a solution of the question which one may refuse to discuss. It does not belong to that class of questions about which people can agree to differ. It is a question for which solution will have to be found. How? It must be by agreement or by arbitration. If it is to be by agreement, it must be the result of negotiations— of give and take and not of surrender by one side to the other. That is not agreement. It is dictation. Good sense may in the end prevail and parties may come to an agreement. But agreement may turn out to be a very dilatory way. It may take long before good sense prevails. How long, one cannot say.

"The political freedom of India is a most urgent necessity. It cannot be postponed and yet without a solution of the communal problem it cannot be hastened. To make it dependent on agreement is to postpone its solution indefinitely. Another expeditious method must be found. It seems to me that arbitration by an International

Board is the best way out. The disputed points in the minorities' problems including that of Pakistan should be remitted to such a Board. The Board should be constituted of persons drawn from the countries outside the British Empire. Each Statutory minority in India – Muslims, Scheduled Castes, Sikhs, Indian Christians – should be asked to select its nominee to this Board of Arbitration. These minorities as also the Hindus should appear before the Board in support of their demands and should agree to abide by the decision given by the Board. The British should give the following undertakings:

"1. They will have nothing to do with the communal settlement. It will be left to agreement or to a Board of Arbitration.

"2. They will implement the decision of the Board of Arbitration on the communal question by embodying it in the Government of India Act.

"3. That the award of the International Board of Arbitration would be regarded by them as a sufficient discharge of their obligations to the minorities in India and would agree to give India Dominion Status.

"The procedure has many advantages. It eliminates the fear of British interference in the communal settlement which has been offered by the Congress as an excuse for its not being able to settle the communal problem. It is alleged that, as there is always the possibility of the minorities getting from the British something more than what the Congress thinks it proper to give, the minorities do not wish to come to terms with the Congress. The proposal has a second advantage. It removes the objections of the Congress that by making the constitution subject to the consent of the minorities, the British Government has placed a veto in the hands of the minorities over the constitutional progress of India. It is complained that the minorities can unreasonably withhold their consent or they can be prevailed upon by the British Government to withhold their consent as the minorities are suspected by the Congress to be mere tools in the hands of the British Government. International Arbitration removes completely every ground of complaint on this account. There should be no objection on the part of the minorities. If their demands are fair and just no minority need have any fear from a Board of International Arbitration. There is nothing unfair in the requirement of a submission to arbitration. It follows the well known rule of law, namely, that no man should be allowed to be a judge in his own case. There is no reason to make any exception in the case of a minority. Like an individual it cannot claim to sit in a judgment over its own case.

What about the British Government? I cannot see any reason why the British Government should object to any part of this scheme. The Communal Award has brought great odium on the British. It has been a thankless task and the British should be glad to be relieved of it. On the question of the discharge of their responsibilities for making adequate provision for the safety and security of communities in respect of which they have regarded themselves as trustees before they relinquish their sovereignty what more can such communities ask than the implementation in the constitution of safeguards in terms of the award of an International Board of Arbitration? There is only one contingency which may appear to create some difficulty for the British Government in the matter of enforcing the award of the Board of Arbitration. Such a contingency can arise if anyone of the parties to the dispute is not prepared to submit its case to arbitration. In that case the question will be: will the British Government be justified in enforcing the award against each party? I see no difficulty in saying that the British Government can with perfect justice proceed to enforce the award against such a party. After all, what is the status of a party which refuses to submit its case to arbitration? The answer is that such a party is an aggressor. How is an aggressor dealt with? By subjecting him to sanctions.

"Implementing the award of the Board of Arbitration in a constitution against a party which refuses to go to arbitration is simply another name for the process of applying sanctions against an aggressor. The British Government need not feel embarrassed in following this process if the contingency should arise. For it is a well recognised process of dealing with such cases and has the imprimatur of the League of Nations which evolved this formula when Mussolini refused to submit to arbitration his dispute with Abyssinia. What I have proposed may not be the answer to the question: What next? I do not know what else could be. All I know is that there will be no freedom for India without an answer. It must be decisive, it must be prompt and it must be satisfactory to the parties concerned." (*Dr. Babasaheb Ambedkar: Writings and Speeches*, Vol. 8, pp. 411-416)

Letter from Durlab Singh

Durlab Singh, a Sikh leader, wrote a letter to Gandhiji on 12 November 1944 in which he said: "The Congress had promised in its Lahore Resolution of 1929 that no constitution would be acceptable to the Congress which does not give the fullest satisfaction to the Sikhs. You know a large number of Sikhs are perturbed over Rajaji's proposals. Supposing Mr. Jinnah had accepted the proposals in full, or in an amended form, what would have been the position of Sikhs in that?

"Even the Akalis feel very indignant, because you did not touch the question of meeting a Sikh deputation as suggested by Master Tara Singh in his letter. Can you please make it clear why it was not considered desirable to invite the Sikh leaders before proceeding to meet Mr. Jinnah for talks?

"Mr. Jagat Narayan Lal's Resolution clearly states that the Congress would be no party to the vivisection of the country. Is it not a fact that Rajaji's proposals run counter to that solution? The Sikh public is made to believe that Gandhiji does not favour the idea of the Sikhs remaining in the Congress because of their belief in the sword.

"Master Tara Singh and other responsible Akali leaders have often declared in the Press and on the platform that the Sikander-Baldev Singh pact was enacted with the consent and blessings of the Congress High Command and Sardar Patel's special representative who was present in the Punjab throughout the negotiations and that the Sardar was kept informed of all the developments. Further, It is said that the Azad Punjab scheme was introduced with your consent and blessings. The nationalist Sikhs regard both the schemes as anti-national and opposed to the interests of the country and the community. Can you kindly guide us in the matter?

"In the end I will request you, Bapuji, to give a general assurance to the nationalist Sikhs that their interests are safe in your hands and that they will not be sacrificed at any cost. The heart of the Sikh masses is with the Congress and nationalism and patriotism are their proud heritage. They cannot depart from these principles, but let them have this satisfaction at least that the Congress will do no injustice to them. And that they will have their proper place in India."

Gandhiji's Reply

Gandhiji sent his letter dated 14 November to Durlab Singh in which he said: "This is my answer to your questions. My association with Rajaji in his formula could not affect the Sikh position in the slightest degree even if Qaid-e-Azam Jinnah accepted it. The Lahore Resolution of the Congress referred to by you stands. The result of Qaid-e-Azam Jinnah's acceptance would have been that both of us would have gone to the Sikhs and others interested to secure their acceptance. I have made this clear in my letter to Masterji (Tara Singh).

"I cannot understand the Akali indignation. My meeting a deputation was unnecessary in view of my absolute assurance. If Masterji wanted to bring his friends to me, in spite of my assurance, I would have gladly seen them as I did other friends who sought clarification from me.

"Maulana Saheb explained the implications of the Jagat Narayan Lal's Resolution which please see. But supposing that is inconsistence with the Rajaji Formula and the Congress accepts the latter, there is nothing to prevent the Congress from rescinding the Resolution.

"How could I favour a contrary opinion when I have always given the closest collaboration to Sikh friends? Those Sikhs, who do not accept the Congress creed, naturally refrain, like many others, from joining the Congress.

"I know nothing about the Sikander-Baldev Singh Pact, much less about the Congress High Command's association with it. Nor do I know the details of the Azad Punjab scheme.

"I could never be guilty of blessing any thing which is contrary to the national interest. You can certainly have the assurance that the interests of the nationalist Sikhs, as also of all nationalists, are safe in my hands, also, I presume, in the Congress hands, though as you know I have no authority to speak on behalf of the Congress.

"There are many inventions about me going the round. I would warn friends against giving credence to any of them without reference to me." (*Collected Works of Mahatma Gandhi,* Vol. 78 pp. 426, 427, 423, 425)

In December 1944, the All-India Hindu Mahasabha met at Bilaspur under the presidentship of Dr. Shyma Prasad Mookherji. Without mincing words, he said emphatically that Pakistan could never be won by the Muslim League on its own strength. He further said: "Jinnah counts on the British support to divide India. If the British sword is to be perpetuated for defending Pakistan, it becomes a colossal hoax and a badge of unbroken slavery."

6

Non-Party Conference

Ever since the breakdown of the Gandhi-Jinnah talks a few of the Hindu and Muslim extremists had been carrying on a bitter controversy over the Pakistan issue, and the use of the words 'civil war' was becoming far too frequent in public speeches. Sir Tej Bahadur Sapru, alarmed at the way in which the communal situation was deteriorating, wrote to Gandhiji suggesting the holding of an all-party conference; but Sir Tej Bahadur himself was doubtful whether his proposal would lead to any satisfactory result and, after some discussion with Gandhiji, the suggestion was dropped. Another proposal was that Gandhiji should call a national convention, but he was not agreeable to doing so. Subsequently, Sir Tej Bahadur suggested to Gandhiji that a Standing Committee of the Non-Party conference should set up a committee and prescribe for it certain duties. The object of this committee would not be to bring about a settlement in the sense that the document would be executed, signed, sealed and delivered, but to understand the point of view of each party and to act as a sort of conciliation board by establishing contacts with the leaders of all parties, and then to recommend such solution as they thought fit. It would be open to the parties to accept it wholly or partially, or to reject it. Gandhiji accepted the suggestion, but said that the members of the committee should not belong to the Congress, the League, the Mahasabha, or any of the recognised parties, and that they should be persons who had not definitely committed themselves to any particular view since the breakdown of the Gandhi-Jinnah talks.

The Standing Committee of the Non-party Conference met on 18 and 19 November 1944, and decided to set up a committee to examine the whole communal and minorities question from a constitutional and political point of view, put itself in touch with the different parties and their leaders, including the minorities interested in the question, and present a solution within two months to the Standing Committee of the Non-party Conference. Sir Tej Bahadur Sapru was authorised to appoint the members of the committee.

Sir Tej Bahadur Sapru held a press conference the same day at which he explained that the proposed committee would consist of people who were not actively associated with any of the recognised political parties and who had not publicly expressed opinion on the political controversy. The committee's object would be to lift the discussion of the communal and political problem from the partisan to the scientific and judicial level. He hoped that two ex-High Court Judges and possibly one or two Englishmen would serve on the committee, which would do all it could to ascertain the views of the various political parties. He said that if any party declined to cooperate, there would be no recriminations, though the fact would be recorded. Sir Tej Bahadur added that he had Gandhiji's support and he hoped that the Government would adopt a reasonable attitude to any approach by the committee for information or statistics.

On December 3, 1944, Sir Tej Bahadur Sapru announced the names of his Conciliation Committee. He said that it was his intention to write to leaders of the various parties and organisations requesting them to agree to personal interviews. The committee would be free to devise its own procedure. It was proposed to publish all important papers along with the report of the committee. The field of the work of the committee was obviously limited. It was not attempting to frame a detailed constitution. Its purpose was to investigate whether there was a possibility of reconciling conflicting views and of suggesting a basis on which a constitutional structure might be built, and for this the committee would welcome and be grateful for help from every quarter.

Shortly after this, Sir Tej Bahadur wrote to Jinnah asking whether he would meet him and one or two other members of the committee with a view to clarifying certain points. Jinnah replied that he could not recognise the committee of the Non-Party Conference, or its Standing Committee, and that he was therefore unable to comply with the request. He added that he did not mean any discourtesy to Sir Tej Bahadur personally; that if the latter had desired to meet him otherwise than on behalf of the Non-Party Conference he would have been glad to see him. Then there was Ambedkar, who was inclined at first to cooperate, but who later withdrew because he disliked the composition of the committee. Despite these rebuffs, the Sapru Committee went ahead with its inquiries.

Sapru Committee's recommendations were published shortly after Lord Wavell's departure to London. The main features were that a national Government should replace the present Executive Council at the Centre; that in the provinces the Congress ministries should resume office but with an admixture of non-Congress parties; that the constitution-making body, representation of Hindus (excluding Scheduled Castes) and Muslims should be equal; that similar parity in the central Assembly should be conditional on Muslims agreeing to joint electorates with reservation of seats instead of separate electorates; and no decision of the constitution-making body should be valid unless it was supported by the three-fourths of the members present and voting, and that His Majesty's Government, while accepting the decisions so made, should supplement them by its own awards where the requisite majority was not obtained. The Committee firmly rejected the Pakistan idea (though two of its members were willing—if no other basis for an agreed settlement were forthcoming—to consider a division of the country, subject to a definite agreement in respect of common matters of defence and economic development.

In spite of the eminent and talented personalities of which it was composed, the Committee failed in its efforts to advance the position. For one thing, the Committee was handicapped by the absence of any top-ranking Muslim. Its rejection of the Pakistan idea and recommendation of joint electorates made the Muslim League's attitude all the more hostile. There was disapproval, even from non-Congress Hindus, who were unable to acquiesce in the proposal for parity between Muslims and Hindus other than the Scheduled Castes.

7

Dr. K.M. Munshi's Compromise Formula

On December 5, Tej Bahadur Sapru requested Dr. K. M. Munshi to send a memorandum to his committee. Munshi sent the draft of memorandum as given below:

"Any solution of the present deadlock has to be essentially a compromise between the fundamental factors which are Britain's suspicions about Congress intentions and fears about her own future in the post-war world, Muslim aspirations for an autonomy free from Hindu domination, Congress insistent on an independent nation-state and the princes' ambitions for their dynastic perpetuation and quasi-sovereignty."

"Such a solution has to proceed from the Constitution Act of 1935 which has given the country institutional integrity. At the same time India has to be divided into three zones—Hindu, Muslim and the zone of the Indian States—with a recognised place for each in the Constitution. The Federal Centre will have jurisdiction in both Concurrent and Federal subjects as regards the Hindu zone, but only in Federal subjects as regards the State Zone and the Muslim Zone also if the Muslim provinces so desire. In the Legislature which will continue to be formed as in the Act of 1935, the Assembly will represent the Union of India, and the Council of State its three zones with equal representation for each. Till the States decide to accede, the Hindu and Muslim zones can constitute the Council.

"This constitutional compromise will thus reflect the three group sentiments which dominate Hindus, Muslims and the Princes. The national bond which will keep them together will be represented by the Assembly and the Ministry responsible to it. The British Indian Muslim zone and the princes' zone will have as great a measure of autonomy as is consistent with a Federal Centre. The fears of the Muslim League and the Princes that their autonomy will be interfered with by the Centre can be removed, if like the Senate of the U.S.A., the Upper House (Council of State) is vested with legislative and executive authority in certain federal matters of vital importance.

"In order to inaugurate such a compromise formula Britain must implement its promise made in the Cripps Offer by a formal Declaration in the parliament that His Majesty's Government intends bringing into existence a Union of India which will constitute a Dominion associated with the United Kingdom and the other Dominions by a common allegiance to the Crown, but equal to them in every respect, and in no way subordinate in any aspect of domestic or external affairs. She must create a healthy atmosphere in the country by a general release of all political prisoners and detenus not implicated in pro-Axis activity. She must restore the normal constitutions in Section 93 Provinces, and reconstitute the Executive Council so as to include therein a majority of members pledged to carry out the Compromise Formula. She must set up a representative Committee to suggest modifications in the Act of 1935 which would carry out the Declaration aforesaid and such other modifications as may be necessary to carry out the Compromise Formula; and decide to bring in the Federal part of the Act as soon as all the Provincial Legislatures begin to function.

"For the purpose of the division of the country into zones, the contiguous areas in the Punjab and Bengal which have an absolute majority of Muslims should be formed into separate Provinces according to the division envisaged in the Rajaji Formula. But differing from it, it is proposed that the areas of the Punjab and Bengal in which Muslims are not in an absolute majority should be formed into separate Provinces unless the non-Muslims in such districts decide in a suitable manner to be included in the Muslim Zone. On the Federal part of the 1935 Act being introduced, the Provinces of the Muslim Zone, by a majority vote in their respective Legislatures, shall be free to decide by an absolute majority that the provisions of the Act which give the Central Legislature power to make laws in respect of the subjects in the Concurrent Legislative List of Schedule VII of the Act shall not apply to them. On such decisions suitable changes shall be made in the Act modifying the said provisions accordingly.

"The Council of State, constituted of 45 members, 15 from each zone, shall be elected by the members of the provincial legislatures in each Hindu and Muslim zone and elected or nominated by the States acceding to the Federation. It will have the power, by a two-thirds vote, of appointing Supreme Court Judges, Ambassadors etc., alter boundaries of States and Provinces, making changes in the Constitution Act, altering the Fundamental Rights of Citizens, introducing or amending Financial Bills, vetoing communal legislation by an absolute majority.

"Ten years after this Compromise Formula is incorporated in the Act and is brought into operation the Constitutional Problem shall be reviewed by a Constituent Assembly of 55 members elected by the Assembly and the members of the Senate sitting as a single house.

"During the transition period of say six months from the time the changes suggested are brought into operation under the Amended Act, all parties must pledge themselves actively to support the war effort. The Congress should support the Formula by forming a parliamentary party of its own to work it or supporting other parties who desire to work it out. At least it should desist from opposing other parties by civil disobedience or otherwise. The Hindu Mahasabha and the Muslim League should give similar support or adopt an attitude of acquiesce.

"The Sapru Committee must immediately convene a Convention which will focus all opinions in the country and become an instrument for securing the support of all parties to the Compromise Formula. With the aid of the Convention it should convert itself into a Centre Party which will draw men anxious for the solution during the Transition Period from all parties and which will secure the support or acquiescence of other parties and interests. If however, the convention is not supported by anyone of the parties or interests concerned, the Centre Party should still continue to work for the Formula by inviting the support of such of them as are willing to do so. If the Congress does not support the Compromise Formula or form a Parliamentary Party, no result whatever could be achieved unless the Sapru Committee or the Convention or the Centre party drops the role of a group of men with high prestige and becomes the nucleus of a dynamic political party with country-wide influence and organisation.

"I realise that the solution of the Indian deadlock is in practice a difficult matter. The Muslim League will not come into any scheme of compromise. The Congress will find it well nigh impossible to jettison its old association. Britain will not abandon her old policies easily. The Sapru Committee may not gather the strength to found a Centre

Party; or the Congress or Britain might destroy the attempt, as they easily can. The deadlock will then continue. Then perhaps another war or more effective mass movements will secure different results." (K.M.Munshi, *Pilgrimage to Freedom,* pp. 426-28)

8

The Bhulabhai Desai-Liaqat Ali Pact

After the failure of the Gandhi-Jinnah talks, Lord Wavell formulated his own plan to end the political deadlock. He decided to invite the political leaders to a conference at Simla. In order to induce His Majesty's Government to accept his proposal, he felt it necessary to proceed to England to discuss the situation with the British cabinet, particularly the Prime Minister, Winston Churchill. Unwittingly Sapru's move delayed the departure of Wavell, who wanted to see the outcome of Sapru's efforts before he proceeded to England.

Wavell was also detained by the abortive attempt made by Bhulabhai Desai, member of the Working Committee and leader of the Congress party in the Central Legislature, to form a coalition Government at the Centre. For this purpose, Bhulabhai had come to an agreement with Liaqat Ali which ran as follows:

1. Desai and Jinnah should be invited to form an Interim Government at the Centre;
2. They would then consult the groups in the Indian Legislature and submit names to the Governor-General for inclusion in the Executive Council. The selection would not be confined to members of the Legislature;

3. Communal proportions within the Council would be settled by agreement. Bhulabhai Desai would be accommodating about this; he said that, speaking for himself if the Muslim League insisted, he would agree to equality between them and the Congress, with a 20 per cent reservation for the rest;
4. The Interim Government would work within the present constitution, but all the members of the Executive Council, except the Governor-General and the Commander-in-Chief, would be Indians;
5. As regards the long term solution, there would be no commitments. The long term solution might be easier when the interim Government had been in office for a year or so;
6. In the provinces, the existing ministries would not be interfered with, though there might be adjustments based on party agreements with which His Majesty's Government would not be concerned. Section 93 administrations would be replaced by coalition ministries including both Congress and League elements;
7. There would be no general elections either at the Centre or in the Provinces;
8. Detenus would not be released before the formation of the interim Central Government.

Desai claimed that these proposals had the support of Gandhiji, that they were based on informal talks with Liaqat Ali Khan, that if the British Government really wanted a Central Government with political background they could get it.

The Viceroy suggested to the Secretary of State that Bhulabhai Desai's plan afforded an excellent opportunity of making progress in the political sphere. It not only accorded with his own proposals, but it had the advantage of being put forward by an Indian.

Meanwhile Jinnah made a public statement disclaiming any knowledge of the Desai-Liaqat Ali Pact. Desai was undeterred by Jinnah's disclaimer and continued to canvass support for his plan. Desai happened to meet V.P. Menon about this time. He told him that no serious notice be taken of Jinnah's disclaimer, which had been expressed in very guarded language; that he himself had acted with the knowledge of Gandhiji and that, if the Government accepted his plan, Jinnah will certainly participate, even though he might express dissatisfaction in public.

Lord Wavell asked Sir John Colville, the Governor of Bombay, to see Jinnah on his behalf, and find out if he thought the Desai proposals worth pursuing and if so, whether he would come to Delhi as soon as possible for discussions with himself and Desai. Sir John Colville saw Jinnah, who stated that he knew nothing about the talks between Desai and Liaqat Ali Khan and that the proposals had been made without any authority from the League. He said that he would be going to Delhi early in March and that he would be glad to discuss the matter with the Viceroy on his arrival. Unfortunately, when Jinnah reached Delhi, he fell ill and was unable to meet the Viceroy.

Desai's formula was an attempt to break the political deadlock on the lines of an ad hoc practical compromise. But Desai was latter repudiated by Jinnah, as well as by the leaders of the Congress, and the ultimate result of his labor was his own political extinction.

Dr. K. M. Munshi, in his book, *Pilgrimage to Freedom,* writes: "During all these negotiations, Bhaulabhai did not realise the full implications of what he was doing on behalf of the Congress. For some time, he did not contradict Liaqat Ali's statement in the Assembly, nor did the steadfast refusal of Jnnnah to meet him awaken him to the risk that he was running. His impatience to reach a settlement with the League led him to ignore Gandhiji's advice to be more circumspect in dealing with Liaqat and to consult the members of the Working Committee.

"Several members of the Working Committee did feel that Bhaulabhai Desai's action in coming to a settlement with Liaqat without securing the release of the members of the Working Committee and without the Congress and the League entering into an alliance, was in the nature of a betrayal. Gandhiji also felt very hurt that his name had been used without authority. Bhaulabai's name was not included in the Congress list of members for the National Government, suggested by the Working Committee at the Simla Conference of July 1945, and in the next general election he was not nominated as a candidate for the Central Assembly."

9

The Simla Conference

Lord Wavell was convinced that the deadlock in India could be broken only by *demarche* by the third party, the British Government or himself as proconsul. He wrote a letter to Winston Churchill on 24h October 1944 in which he said: "...If India is not to be ruled by force, it must be ruled by the heart rather than by hear. I am prepared to put up proposals for a move, which will involve risks, but which I think constitute the best chance of making progress. If we are to make any progress, we must take risks and be prepared for the failure; but a move made generously and honestly, even if it failed, it would be good."

Having received no reply from Churchill, Wavell sent a reminder on 15 March 1945, in response to which he was summoned to London on 25 March 1945. After prolonged discussions, he obtained permission to make announcement of his proposals on behalf of His Majesty's Government, which he did on 14 June after his return to India. Wavell's proposals, among other things contained reconstitution of Viceroy's Executive Council with Indian leaders, caste Hindus and Muslims being equally represented. On the same day Amery, the Secretary of State, announced in the British parliament that the Viceroy would convene a conference of Indian leaders to break the deadlock.

The Viceroy convened the conference at Simla on 25 June, to which he invited 21 leaders of various shades. The Congress Working Committee authorised Gandhi and Azad to attend the conference.

The Simla Conference began with the introductory remarks from the Viceroy. He said: "What was proposed was not a constitutional settlement or a final solution of India's problems, nor did the plan in anyway prejudge or prejudice the final issue. But if it succeeded, it would pave the way towards a settlement.

"The statesmanship, wisdom and goodwill of all of us, is here on trial, not merely in the eyes of India, but before the whole world. It was necessary to rise above the level of old prejudices and enmities and of party and sectional advantages and to think of the good of the four hundred million people of India."

Wavell asked the members to believe in him as a sincere friend of India and as one who would endeavour to guide the discussions of the conference in what he believed to be the best interest of the country.

Referring to the Viceroy's announcement, Gandhiji said: "It is a good and dignified expression that Lord Wavell has used. He thus acts in the conference as its leader and not as the agent of Whitehall."

By the second day, the conference agreed on certain principles like representation for minorities, wholehearted support to the war efforts and continuance of Viceroy's reconstituted Executive Council under the Government of India Act 1935 till the end of the war. Differences, however, arose about the composition of the Executive Council. Jinnah's demand was that the Congress could nominate all the Hindu members, but all the Muslim members must be the nominees of the Muslim League. Azad vehemently opposed and said: "Congress had approached all political problems from a national point of view and recognised no distinction between Hindus and Muslims on political issues." It could not in any circumstances agree to be an organisation of Hindus only. The Congress should have freedom to nominate any Indian it liked regardless of whether he was a Hindu or a Muslim or a Christian, or a Parsi, or a Sikh. Congress should participate on the basis of Indian nationhood or not participate at all. So far as the Muslim League was concerned, it was for it to decide who should be its nominees.

Jinnah expressed a wish that he would like to have an informal discussion with the Congress. Azad nominated for this purpose Govind Vallabh pant, whom he thought would be the right person to negotiate with Jinnah. (*Maulana Abul Kalam Azad, India Wins Freedom,* pp. 116-17)

The Viceroy suggested that Jinnah and Azad should meet in the presence of Richardson, the leader of the European Group, and himself. Jinnah avoided it by saying that he and Govind Vallabh Pant would be meeting and so there was no necessity for his meeting Azad. When Pant went to meet, Jinnah asked him if he had any fresh proposal to make. On the former saying he had none, the meeting ended.

When the conference met on 29 June, the Viceroy announced that since the parties were unable to come to an agreement, he would use his personal offices to resolve the differences. He asked all interests represented in the conference to send him the list of persons they would like to be selected for joining the National Government. He would add to them some names himself and after scrutinising all the names, he would try to arise at a list which would be generally acceptable to the conference.

Jinnah was not agreeable to this proposal. He first wanted to know whether, if the League sent a list, the Viceroy would accept the League panel *en bloc.* The Viceroy replied that he could not give such guarantee beforehand.

Jinnah next asked whether the Viceroy would still proceed with his proposal if one of the parties finally rejected it, to which again the Viceroy replied that he could not commit himself in advance as to what he would do in the contingency envisaged.

Finally, when the Viceroy asked Jinnah pointblank whether the League would submit the list of names or not, Jinnah answered that he was there only in his individual capacity; he would need the Viceroy's proposal in writing to place before the Working Committee of the League before he could give a definite reply. He was told that he would have it.

Jinnah wrote to Wavell: "With regard to your suggestion for submitting a panel of names, the Working Committee of the Muslim League desires to point out that when a similar proposal was made by your Excellency's predecessor, Lord Linlithgow, the Working Committee opposed it and, when its objections were brought to the notice of Linlithgow, he dropped the proposal and suggested another alternative." Lord Linlithgow's alternative was contained in the following letter of 25 September 1940: "I am contained that the selection of the representatives, while resting with the Governor General, be based in the case of the Muslim League not on a panel formally submitted but on confidential discussion between the leader of the party concerned and myself (Viceroy)."

Concluding his letter, Jinnah wrote: "The Working Committee is of the opinion that the procedure settled on the previous occasion should be followed in the presence case so far as the Muslim League is concerned." (*Pyarelal, Mahatma Gandhi—Last Phase, Vol. II,* pp. 135-36)

By 7 July the Congress and the minor parties submitted their lists to the Viceroy. Congress list was a recommendation for the composition of the Council as a whole; it therefore, included representatives of all major parties, including Jinnah and two other members of the League; and the names of only five Congressmen were submitted, two of whom were Azad and Asaf Ali.

Azad made it explicit that the inclusion of those two Muslims in the Congress panel was a matter of principle. He said: "The Congress is essentially a national organisation, and cannot possibly a party to any arrangement, howsoever, temporary it may be, that prejudices its national character and tends to impair its growth of nationalism, and reduces the Congress indirectly to a communal body." (*D.G. Tendulkar, Mahatma,* Vol. VII, p. 10)

On 11 July, Wavell saw Jinnah again and told him that he was prepared to include in the Council four members of the Muslim League, together with a non-League Muslim from the Punjab, all of whom he named, asking that if Jinnah wanted to substitute other League names he would consider them – indeed he would be glad if Jinnah himself would serve. But Jinnah refused even to discuss the names unless he could be given the absolute right to select all Muslims and some guarantee that any decision which the Muslims opposed in the Council could only be passed by a two-third majority-in fact a kind of communal veto. Wavell told Jinnah that these conditions were entirely unacceptable.

At the last meeting of the conference on 14 July, Jinnah claimed parity inside the Council with all other parties combined. "If he really meant this," commented Wavell, "it shows that Jinnah had never at any time an intention of accepting the offer, and it is difficult to see why he came to Simla at all." (*Anita Inder Singh, The Origins of the Partition of India*, pp. 122-23)

Wavell did not want the conference to break down. He proposed to send his own list of nominees to Amery for approval. He then wanted to show the list to Jinnah and other party leaders. If either the League or the Congress or both rejected the list he would close the conference and disclose the names put forward by him in a broadcast.

At the last session of the conference on 14 July, the Viceroy made a statement accepting the full responsibility for the failure of the conference. He said: "On 29 June I undertook, with the approval of the conference, to endeavor to produce a solution not based on any formula agreed in advance. I asked the parties to let me have lists of names, and said that I would do what I could to produce a solution acceptable to the leaders and the conference.

"I received lists from all parties represented here except from the European Group (who decided not to send a list) and the Muslim League. I was, however, determined that the conference should not fail until I have made every possible effort to bring it to a successful ending. I therefore, made my provisional selections including certain Muslim League names, and I have every reason to believe that if these selections had been acceptable here, they would have been acceptable to His Majesty's Government.

"My selection would, I think, have given a balanced and efficient Executive Council, whose composition would have been reasonably fair to all parties. I did not find it possible, however, to accept the claims of any party in full.

When I explained my solution to Jinnah, he told me that it was not acceptable to the Muslim League, and he was so decided that I felt it would be useless to continue the discussions. In the circumstances, I did not show my selection as a whole to Jinnah and there was no object in showing them to the other leaders.

"The conference has therefore failed. Nobody can regret this more than I do myself. I wish to make it clear that the responsibility for the failure is mine. The main idea underlying the conference was mine. If it had succeeded, its success would have been attributed to me, and I cannot place the blame for its failure upon any of the parties. I ask the party leaders to accept this view, and to do all they can to ensure that there are no recriminations. It is of the utmost importance that this effort to secure agreement between the parties and communities should not result in a worsening of communal feeling. I ask you all to exercise the greatest possible restraint." (V.P.Menon, *The Transfer of Power in India,* pp. 242-43)

"It gives me to think," wrote Gandhiji in his final letter to the Viceroy, "that the conference which began so happily and so hopefully should have ended in apparent failure due to exactly, as it would seem, to the same cause as before. This time you have taken the blame on your own shoulders. But the world would think otherwise. India certainly does." Probing into the cause of failure, Gandhiji continued: "I must not hide from me the suspicion, that the deeper cause is perhaps the reluctance of the official world, to part with power, which the passing of virtual control into the hands of their erstwhile princes would have meant."

Jinnah in a statement characterised the Wavell plan as a snair and a death warrant for the Muslim League because, even if all the Muslims in the Government were to be the Muslim Leaguers, they would still be in minority of one-third in the Cabinet. "The representatives of all the minorities," Jinnah said, "would in actual practice, invariably vote against us in the Government." Previously, Jinnah used to say that the Muslim League was the champion and protector of all the minorities in India, and the Congress represented not even Hindus but caste Hindus only. But now he said: "All other minorities, such as Scheduled Castes, Sikhs, and Christians have the same goal as the Congress. Their goal and ideology is of a united India. Ethnically and culturally, they are very closely knitted to Hindu society."

In the opinion of Maulana Abul Kalam Azad: "The Simla conference marks a breakwater in Indian political history. This was the first time when the negotiations failed, not on the basic political issue dividing different Indian groups.

"If, the conference had not broken down because of Jinnah's opposition, the result would have been that Muslims who constitute only about 25 % of the total population of India, would have had seven representatives in the Council of fourteen. This is evidence of the generosity of the Congress and also throws in lurid light the stupidity of the Muslim League. The League was supposed to be the guardian of Muslim interests and yet it was because of its opposition that the Muslims of India were denied a substantial share in the Government of Undivided India." (Maulana Abul Kalam Azad, *India Wins Freedom,* pp. 123-24)

"In a province, " wrote Aazd, "where Muslims were in a majority, there was no League Ministry. There was a Congress Ministry in the Frontier Province. In Bengal, there was Governor's rule, while in the Punjab, it was Unionist Ministry. In Sind, Sir Ghulam Hussain depended on Congress support and the same position held in Assam. It could not, therefore, be claimed that the Muslim League represented all Muslims. There was in fact, a large block of Muslims who had nothing to do with the League." (V.B. Kulkarni, *The Indian Triumvirate,* pp. 192)

Jawaharlal Nehru said: "The Muslim League represented medieval concept and fear complex and that India one day would have to settle the problem of communalism if she wished to progress as a modern democratic State. The old concept of Nation State was now outmoded and that the real modern problems lay in the economic sphere."

V.P. Menon, who functioned as Secretary of the conference, in his book, *Transfer of Power in India,* says: "I personally was terribly disappointed, for I had been pressing consistently on the Viceroy that Jinnah's claim that the Muslim League represented the will of all Muslims of India was quite untenable; that we could not let down the Unionist party which alone contrary to the League's claim, could speak for the Punjab; that in the interest of the Punjab, we should not compromise with the League, but should go ahead with our plans. My argument was that if we conceded Jinnah's claims, we should logically be conceding his demand for Pakistan. Even on that basis, the Muslim league should not be entitled to a great standing than that which was due to a future State of Pakistan, which could not possibly claim to represent the millions of non-Muslims in the non-Pakistan areas of India. But the decision not to proceed with the proposals, we were told, was final and there was nothing more to be said."

Menon further says: "Just before the Viceroy communicated his final decision to the members, Hossain Imam, who attended the conference in his capacity as a leader of the Muslim League party in the Council of State stopped me on my way to the Cecil Hotel and confided to me his feeling of distress over the imminent breakdown. He urged me even at that late hour to see Liaqat Ali Khan in order to find a way out of the impasse. He gave me the impression that the members of the Working Committee of the Muslim League were far from unanimous in rejecting the Viceroy's offer. Hossain Imam suggested that the Viceroy was not aware that a member of his own Executive Council was advising Jinnah to stand firm.

"The abandonment of the plan undoubtedly strengthened the position of Jinnah and the League at a time when their fortunes were none too good. It weakened the position of those Muslims who had been opposing the League, particularly the Unionist party in the Punjab, and since it was clear that Jinnah could alone deliver the goods, the wavering and middle-of-the-road Muslim politicians tended to gravitate to the Muslim League." (V. P. Menon, *The Transfer of Power in India,* pp. 249-50)

K.M. Munshi in his book, *Pilgrimage to Freedom* at page 96 writes: "The Simla conference changed the course of our political development. The British Government lost its initiative and was hardly counted as a party to any political settlement. Wavell's personal prestige declined. The Congress, which had made the genuine attempt to make the conference a success lost whatever faith it had in the British Government. Jinnah's position as the sole determining factor in India's political fortunes, however, remained unshaken."

Jinnah blamed all except himself and his men for the failure of the Simla conference. He also insulted Maulana Azad by calling him, "a Muslim show-boy Congress President." It became axiomatic with him that all those who were not with him were against him.

J.P. Menon in his book, *Transfer of Power in India* at page 251 says: "The Simla conference afforded a last opportunity to the forces of nationalism to fight a rear-guard section to preserve the integrity of the country, and when the battle was lost the waves of communalism quickly engulfed it. Only the Hobson's choice of partition was left." And this is what Jinnah had aimed at. He drove the conference to terminate in failure. The later events led to the appointment of the Cabinet Mission.

10

The Cabinet Mission

Lord Pethic Lawrence, the Secretary of State for India made the following statement in the House of Lords on 19 February 1946: "....In view of the paramount importance, not only to India and to the British Commonwealth but to the peace of the world, the British Government have decided with the approval of His Majesty to send to India a special mission of Cabinet Ministers consisting of Lord Pethic Lawrence, the Secretary of State for India, Sir Stafford Cripps, the President of the Board of Trade, and Mr. A.V. Alexander, the First Lord of the Admiralty, to act in association with the Viceroy in this matter."

The Cabinet Mission arrived in Delhi on 24 March 1946. They interviewed 472 Indian leaders in 182 sittings. In all these interviews and discussions, there loomed the one outstanding issue, underlining the difference of approach between the Congress and the Muslim League—a united India vs Pakistan.

The Congress case was presented by Azad. He said that the future constitution would be determined by the constitution-making body and, in the intervening period, there should be an Interim Government at the Centre. On the completion of the work of the constitution-making, a province should have three choices: To stand out of the constitution; to enter the constitution by federating for the compulsory subjects only; and to federate for the compulsory as well as for the optional subjects.

Arguing against the Muslim League demand, Azad stated that autonomy with regard to political subjects could be granted, but the Congress could never agree to the partition of India.

Gandhiji told the Cabinet Mission: "He had never been able to appreciate the Pakistan demanded by Jinnah. Rajaji Formula, if put into shape, should serve as the basis for negotiations; and unless he himself were to be reasoned into it, he could not go further, beyond that Pakistan was an untruth." Gandhiji further said: "In his view the two-nation theory was most dangerous. The Muslim population, but for a microscopic minority was a population of converts. They were all descendents of India-born people."

Gandhiji suggested that Jinnah should be asked to form the first Government with personnel chosen from the electcd members of the Legislature. The Viceroy would appoint them formally, but, in fact, Jinnah would choose them. If Jinnah refused, then the offer to form the Government should be made to the Congress.

To this, Jinnah's reply was: "The Congress offer to serve under his leadership is complete humbug. The Congress had always insisted that such a Government should be responsible to a legislature, which meant that it would be quickly withdrawn. It would not work at all. We should be fighting like Killkenny cats all the times." (Anita Inder Singh, *The Origins of the Partition of India,* p. 155)

Jinnah was invited by the Cabinet Mission to justify his demand for Pakistan. Jinnah told the Cabinet Mission: "Though throughout the history, from the days of Chandragupta, there had never been any Government of India in the sense of single Government. After the British had come, they had gradually established their rule in a large part of India, but even then the country had only been partly united. The Indian States had been separate and sovereign. It was said that India was one, but this was not so. India was really many and was held by the British as one. The Muslims had different conception of the life from the Hindus. They admired different qualities in their heroes; they had a different culture based on Arabic and Persian instead of Sanskrit origins. The social customs ere entirely different. Hindu society and the philosophy were the most exclusive in the world....There were in India two totally different and deeply rooted civilisations side by side, and the only solution was to have two steel frames, one in Hindustan and the one in Pakistan."

The Cabinet Mission interviewed both Jinnah and Azad again with a view to exploring the possibilities of a compromise.

Jinnah was entirely immovable on his demand for Pakistan. He remained firmly opposed to a common legislature of executive, even on the basis of equal representation.

Lord Pethic Lawrence wrote a letter to the President of the Congress and the Muslim League on 27 April requesting them to send four negotiators to meet the Cabinet Mission and the Viceroy to explore the possibility of agreement upon a scheme based upon the following fundamental principles.

The future constitutional structure of the British India to be as follows:

"A Union Government dealing with Foreign Affairs; Defence and Communications. There will be two groups of provinces, the one of the predominantly Hindu provinces and the other of the predominantly Muslim provinces, dealing with all other subjects which the provinces in the respective groups desire to be dealt with common. The provincial governments will deal with all other subjects and they will have all the residuary sovereign rights."

Azad sent his detailed reply on 28 April which he concluded saying: "While we are ready to carry on negotiations with any party, as to the future of India, we must state our conviction that reality will be absent from any negotiations whilst an outside ruling power still exists in India."

The Muslim League agreed to participate in the conference without commitment or prejudice to its position as set forth in its Lahore Resolution of 1940 on Pakistan.

The Congress also agreed to participate in the conference.

The Simla Conference began on 5 May 1946. After two days of discussions, the gulf between the Congress and the League was still as wide as ever. On 8 May Lord Pethic Lawrence suggested certain points for agreement between the representatives of the Congress and the League.

Jinnah protested that the points were a fundamental departure from the original formula proposed by the Secretary of State; that there were many objectionable features in the new suggestions and that no useful purpose will be served by a discussion of them.

Azad also pointed out that some of he suggestions were entirely opposed to the views of the Congress.

Nevertheless, the suggested points for agreement were taken up for discussion when the conference met on 9 May. Nehru suggested that an umpire may be appointed to settle the points of disputes. Jinnah agreed to this. But when the conference met on 11 May, he refused to accept the decision of the umpire. There upon each of the parties was asked to furnish a statement setting out its attitude on the points that were still outstanding.

The Muslim League submitted a memorandum setting out its minimum demands, by way of an offer. The Congress also suggested its points as a basis for agreement.

The differences of views between the Congress and the League provided no hope for reaching any settlement. However, the conference met as scheduled on 12 May and came to the conclusion that no useful purpose would be served by further discussion and therefore announced that the conference has failed to bring the Congress and the Muslim League to agreement.

The Cabinet Mission and the Viceroy published their statements on 16 May 1946. The publication of the Cabinet Mission's statement was followed by a broadcast by the Secretary of State.

Gandhiji was the first to come out with his reaction. He said: "The Cabinet Mission and the Viceroy had tried to bring all the parties together, but they could not bring about an agreement." He likened the announcement to a promissory note, whose worth depended entirely on its genuineness and validity. "If the promise inscribed on a promissory note is not honoured," he said, "the promissory note is worth nothing and fit only to be torn to pieces and thrown away."

Jinnah described the Cabinet Mission statement as cryptic with several lacunas. He regretted that the Cabinet Mission should have ignored 'the League's demand for Pakistan, which was the only solution of the constitutional problems of India and which alone could secure stable Government and lead to the happiness and welfare, not only of the two major communities, but of all the people of Indian sub-continent.

The Viceroy subsequently invited Nehru and Jinnah for a joint consultation. Jinnah replied that until the Congress had given its decision on long term plan of 16 May, no purpose would be served by any discussion on the nature and composition of the interim Government. The joint consultation did not, therefore, take place.

On 12 June, the Viceroy saw Nehru. Nehru suggested there should be 15 members in the interim Government including five Congress (all Hindus), four Muslim League, one non-League Muslim, one non-Congress Hindu, one Congress Scheduled caste, one Indian Christian, one Sikh and one Congress woman.

Wavell expressed his inability to negotiate on this basis, which he felt would be entirely unacceptable to Jinnah.

A complete deadlock was thus reached. The Cabinet Mission and the Viceroy finally issued a statement setting out their own proposals for the composition of an Interim Government.

The Congress Working Committee met on 25 June to deliberate on the Cabinet Mission Plan. Gandhiji advised wholesale rejection of the plan. Azad, Nehru and Sardar were for compromise. In the end, the committee only partially agreed with Gandhiji. It rejected the proposal for the formation of an interim Government at the Center, but accepted the long term proposal of constitution-making with its own interpretation of disputed clauses.

The Working Committee's decision was communicated to the Cabinet Mission. It treated the Congress decision as an acceptance of their Plan of 16 May.

The Cabinet Mission informed Jinnah that the Congress accepted the statement of 16 May and that since both the Congress and the League had now accepted the statement, it was proposed to set up a coalition Government including both parties as soon as possible.

The negotiations for an Interim Government, however, failed. Meanwhile the existing Executive Council had lost some of its members by resignation, so it became necessary to make transitional arrangement at the Center pending further negotiations with the parties. Accordingly, the Viceroy decided to set up a care taker Government composed of officials, who would function until such time as his efforts with the political leaders could be renewed.

The Cabinet Mission left India on 29 June after a stay of more than three months.

Jinnah again succeeded in his designs to drive British and the Congress for the partition of India. He was playing his tactics with the both. He wanted nothing short of Pakistan.

11
The Interim Government

The Congress Working Committee's resolution accepting the Cabinet Mission Plan was submitted to the All India Congress Committee on 6 July 1946 in Bombay for ratification. It was ratified by overwhelming majority.

At this session of the All India Congress Committee, Jawaharlal Nehru was installed as Congress President in place of Maulana Abul Kalam Azad.

Winding up the proceedings Nehru said: "...It was not a question of Congress accepting any plan long or short. It was merely a question of their agreeing to enter the Constituent Assembly and nothing more than that. They would remain in the Constituent Assembly so long as they thought that it was for India's good and they would come out when they thought it was injuring their cause. We are not bound by a single thing except that we have decided for the moment to go to the Constituent Assembly."

With regard to the question of grouping Nehru said: "...There is going to be finally no grouping, because Assam will not tolerate it under any circumstances. Thus grouping business approached from any point of view, does not get us on at all." Jinnah characterised Nehru's statement as a complete repudiation of the basic form on which the long-term plan rests and all its fundamentals and terms and obligations and rights of parties accepting the plan. He further said: "In view of the true intentions of the Congress as expressed in Nehru's statement, it was no longer possible to work in cooperation with the Congress, and therefore, the League had no alternative but to adhere once more to the national goal of Pakistan." He recalled that throughout the negotiations with the Cabinet Mission the other two parties, the British and the Congress, each held a pistol in their hand, the one of authority and arms and the other of mass struggle and non-cooperation. "Today, we have also forged a pistol and we are in a position to use it."

The Viceroy had been in correspondence with the Secretary of State on the subject of the formation of an Interim Government to replace the caretaker Government at the Centre. He wrote a letter to the President of the Congress and the Muslim League on 22 July, which he concluded by saying: "We should not spend further time in negotiations; but should try out a Government at once. If it does not work, and if you find the conditions uneasy, it will be open to you to withdraw, but I am confident that you will not."

The Viceroy invited Nehru on 6 August as Congress President to submit proposals for the formation an Interim Government.

Nehru submitted a list of 12 members for the Interim Government. Two names were left to be filled by the Muslim League; if and when they joined the Government. On 24 August, a press communiqué was issued stating that the King had accepted the resignations of the existing members of the Viceroy's Executive Council and that His majesty had been pleased to appoint in their places the following: "Pandit Jawaharlal Nehru,

Sardar Vallabhbhai patel, Dr. Rajendra Prasad, Mr. Asaf Ali, C. Rjagopalachariar, Sarat Chandra Bose, Dr. John Mathai, Sardar Baldev Sing, Sir Shafaat Ahmed Khan, Syd Ali Zaheer and C.H.Bhaba. Two more Muslim members would be appointed later. The Interim Government would take office on 2 September. The Interim Government was sworn in on 2 September."

On 7 September, Nehru broadcast from the All India Radio in which he said that the Interim Government was a part of a larger scheme, which included the Constituent Assembly. The Constituent Assembly would soon be meeting to give shape to the constitution of free and independent India.

Jinnah gave an interview to the *London Daily Mail* on 8 September. Referring to Nehru's broadcast, he said: "Nehru has made no definite proposals to me; I have been stabbed and kind words will not stop the bleeding."

The Viceroy continued his efforts to bring about a settlement with Nehru and Jinnah. On 13 October, Jinnah wrote to the Viceroy: "...In the interest of Musalmans and other communities it would be fatal to leave the entire field of administration of the Central Government in the hands of the Congress. Besides, you may be forced to have in your Interim Government Muslims who do not command respect and confidence of Muslim India, which would lead to various serious consequences; and lastly, for other very weighty grounds and reasons which are obvious and need not be mentioned, we have decided to nominate five members on behalf of the Muslim League in terms of your broadcast and your two letters to me embodying clarifications and assurances."

On 25 October, names of the Muslim League members of the Interim Government along with their portfolios were announced.

Interim Government was born in an atmosphere of suspicion and distrust between the Congress and the Muslim League and it went on increasing. The League members of the Executive Council behaved and functioned as if Pakistan had already become *fait accompli*. One of them declared that the events in East Bengal, were but a dress rehearsal for his party's countrywide struggle to force India's division. Isphani, Jinnah's personal envoy in America said: "The League's participation only means that the struggle for Pakistan will now be carried on within as well as without the Government." From the start, the League members acted as a parallel Government and ignored Nehru's status as Vice President of the Council. Jinnah publicly said: "If he (Nehru) can only come down to earth and think coolly and calmly, he must understand that he is neither the Prime Minister nor is it a Nehru Government. He is only the member of the External Affairs and Communications Department." The coalition Government was a house at war.

Gandhiji declared that the League's entry into the Interim Government had not been straight. He was forced to wonder whether the League members had come into the Government also to fight.

12

The Mountbatten Plan

Prime Minister Mr. Clement Attlee announced on 20 February 1947 that Britain would transfer power to Indian hands before June 1948. He also announced that Lord Mountbatten would succeed Lord Wavell.

Mountbatten arrived in Delhi on 22 March 1947 with plenipotentiary powers from His Majesty's Government and was sworn in as the Viceroy and Governor General on 24 March.

The first task that confronted Mountbatten was to resolve the crisis within the Interim Government. The second problem was to bring about a truce between Hindus and Muslims.

In the very first meeting with the Viceroy, Gandhiji suggested to ask Jinnah to form the Government to avert partition of the country. Gandhiji strove with the Congress Working Committee for the acceptance of his suggestion made by him to Lord Mountbatten. All except Azad told Gandhiji that the partition was inescapable.

Gandhiji wrote to Mountbatten on 11 April 1947: "...I have several talks with Pandit Nehru and hour's talk with him alone; and then several members of the Working Committee about the formula I had sketched before you. I am sorry to say that I have failed to carry any one of them with me except Badsha Khan. I therefore, ask you to omit me from your consideration."

In the course of his talks with the party leaders, particularly Jinnah, Mountbatten was convinced that there was no prospect of an agreed solution on the basis of the Cabinet Mission Plan and attempt to resurrect it was useless. So an alternative plan for the transfer of power had to be found and implemented without loss of time, in order to ease the growing political tension. Accordingly, he drew up an alternative plan.

The plan provided that the members of the Legislative Assemblies of Bengal and the Punjab should meet separately in two parts, i.e. representatives of the predominantly Muslim areas, and representatives of the predominantly non-Muslim areas, and if both sections of each of these Assemblies voted for partition of Bengal, the predominantly Muslim district of Sylhet in Assam would have the option of joining the Muslim province. The plan also envisaged the holding of election in the North-West Frontier Province to ascertain the wishes of the people of that province.

Jinnah issued a statement that the proposal for the partition of Bengal and the Punjab was a sinister move actuated by spite of bitterness. He suggested that an exchange of population would sooner or later have to take place and that this could be effectively carried out by respective Governments in Pakistan and Hindustan. He finally demanded the division of the Defence forces and stressed that the States of Pakistan and Hindustan should be made absolutely free, independent and sovereign.

In the face of the progressively deteriorating situation in the country, Mountbatten felt that if the procedure for the transfer of power was not finalised quickly, there was a possibility that at least in some parts of the country, there would be no authority to whom power could be transferred. He revised his tentative plan and sent it to London with Lord Ismay and George Allen Campbell on 2 May 1947.

Mountbatten received back his plan from London on 8 May as finalised and approved by the British Cabinet. A press communiqué was issued to the effect that the Viceroy had invited Nehru, Jinnah, Patel, Liaqat Ali Khan, Baldev Singh to meet him in Delhi on the morning of 17 May, when he would present to them the plan which His Majesty's Government had approved for the transfer of power to Indian hands. He also invited the members of the State's Negotiating Committee to meet him on the same afternoon.

On the night of 10 May, Mountbatten showed the Plan to Nehru. Nehru turned it down most vehemently and made it clear that the Congress would under no circumstances accept it.

Mountbatten held a meeting with Nehru. He explained to him as to how the new plan would meet his objections. At the end of the meeting Mountbatten asked Nehru whether the Congress would accept a plan based on their discussions. Nehru replied that he would have to see the draft befcre he could commit himself.

In view of this new development, it was decided that the conference of the party leaders which had been summoned to meet on 17 May, should be postponed to 2 June and a communiqué to that effect was issued.

Mountbatten returned to Delhi from Simla on 14 May. Immediately on his arrival in Delhi, he received an invitation from the Prime Minister to go to London.

Mountbatten felt that he should get consent of the leaders of the three parties to the alternative plan before leaving for London. He asked V.P. Menon to prepare a draft, "Heads of Agreement," to be shown to the leaders for their acceptance. After Mountbatten approved the draft, "Heads of Agreement," Menon took it to Nehru, Patel and Baldev Singh and had discussions with them; Sir Eric Mieville did likewise with Jinnah and Liaqat Ali Khan. Thereafter, Mountbatten consulted Nehru, Patel on behalf of the Congress; Jinnah and Liaqat Ali on behalf of the League; and Baldev Singh on behalf of the Sikhs. In the light of their discussions the new plan was finalised.

On 18 May, Mountbatten left for London. Menon accompanied him. The British Cabinet approved the new plan and finalised the statement of His Majesty's Government. It was decided that Mountbatten should present this plan to the Indian leaders on 2 June. Mountbatten returned to India on 31 May 1947.

13
India Partitioned

The historic conference was held on 2 June 1947 at the Viceroy's house. It was attended by seven leaders namely, Nehru, Patel and Kriplani on behalf of the Congress; Jinnah, Liaqat Ali Khan and Abdur Rab Nashtar on behalf of the League; and Baldev Singh representing the Sikhs.

Copies of the statement of His Majesty's Government were handed over to the leaders. Mountbatten asked the leaders to take the copies to their working committees, to discuss the statement with them that day and let him know their reaction by midnight.

The Congress Committee decided to accept the plan. Jinnah did not give any thing in writing, but assured Mountbatten that he would do all in his power to get the plan accepted. The next morning the Viceroy's conference with leaders was summoned. He told the leaders that he had received written assurances from the Congress and the Sikhs and a verbal assurance from the Muslim League.

Immediately after his meeting with the leaders, the Viceroy communicated to the Secretary of State the assurances given to him by Nehru, Jinnah and Baldev Singh in regard to the acceptance of plan. Attlee announced the plan on 3 June, hence it came to be known as 3 June Plan.

In a broadcast, which the Prime Minister made that night, he said: "As the Indian leaders have finally failed to agree on the Cabinet Mission Plan for a United India, partition becomes inevitable alternative.... The Plan, he added, provided for the handing over of power that year to one or two Governments, each having Dominion Status."

On the evening of 3 June, the Viceroy in his broadcast over All India Radio said that with reasonable goodwill between communities, a united India would be by far the best solution; but it had been impossible to obtain agreement on the Cabinet Mission Plan or on any other plan that would preserve the unity of India. The Muslim League had demanded the partition of India and the Congress had used the same argument for demanding, in the event, the partition of certain provinces. The argument seemed unassailable, though he was as much opposed to the partition of provinces as he was to the partition of India. Hence it was left to the people of India themselves to decide the question of partition.

Immediately thereafter, His Majesty's Government's Statement was also broadcast and released to the press. There followed broadcast by Nehru, Jinnah and Baldev Singh indicating their acceptance of the plan.

The All India Congress Committee met on 14 June and passed a resolution accepting the 3 June plan. Thus India was divided in two sovereign States of Hindustan and Pakistan.

It would be seen that during the talks with Gandhiji for 18 days, Jinnah had insisted on the acceptance of the Muslim League's Lahore resolution of 1940 for the settlement of the Hindu-Muslim problem. Jinnah continued his insistence in the Simla Conference, before the Cabinet Mission and Lord Mountbatten with increasing vehemence and succeeded in getting Pakistan, which was his ultimate goal. In the process, he made father of the Nation miserable and made him yield to the vivisection of India, which he had considered a sin.

The partition of India satisfied the ego of Jinnah and fulfilled the ambition of Nehru to become the first Prime Minister of independent India. But between the two, people suffered beyond measure. The partition has neither brought Hindu-Muslim harmony, nor peace in both the countries-India and Pakistan. There is hardly any hope that India and Pakistan would live as good neighbors. Dr. B.R. Ambedkar had said that the Partition will not bring harmony between the Hindus and Muslims. The relations between the Hindus and Muslims in India and the Indo-Pak relations during the last 62 years proved Dr. Ambedkar prophetic.

Index